The Authors

Maralene and Miles Wesner are multi-talented teachers and prolific writers. They have published more than 150 Audio-Visual Education aids, and pioneered new reading methods with their Phonics in a Nutshell (1965).

They have written articles, and mission studies for Southern Baptist periodicals. They were in the original group of writers to develop WMU's Big "A" Club material.

They've published several books with Broadman Press: *A Fresh Look at the Gospel* (1983); *You Are What You Choose* (1984); and *How To Be a Saint When You Feel Like a Sinner* (1986) and self-published 30 books by Diversity Press.

They are noted for their no-nonsense style, their clear illustrations, and their willingness to face controversial issues. From the dual perspectives of both academic and religious professions, they seek to be a bridge between the spiritual and the intellectual worlds.

They hold Masters Degrees (MEd) from Oklahoma University plus work toward a Doctorate. Miles also attended Southwestern Baptist Theological Seminary, and served as a high school counselor. He has been the bi-vocational pastor of a small rural church for more than 50 years.

Both Maralene and Miles taught in public school and collages and served as educational consultants. Maralene taught Psychology and Speech for Southeastern Oklahoma State University for 32 years. She was chosen Oklahoma Teacher of the Year in 1975.

They have planned, led tours, and done research in all of the 50 states, Canada, Mexico, Europe, Egypt, Japan, and the Holy Land. In 1985, they were among a small group of Americans who were invited by Dr. Joseph P. Kennedy of the US/China Education Foundation and Bishop Ting, leader of the Three Self Movement, to participate in the First Symposium on the Church in Nanjing, China.

Now, they use their lifetime of varied experiences to write insightful sermons, essays, and books.

Titles by Maralene & Miles Wesner
published by Nurturing Faith

Sermons for Special Days

Life More Abundant

Do You Really Know Jesus?

If Jesus Were Here Today

101 Sparks of Inspiration

WHEN GOD CAN'T
Answer

Maralene & Miles Wesner

© 2022
Published in the United States by Nurturing Faith, Macon, GA.
Nurturing Faith is a book imprint of Good Faith Media (goodfaithmedia.org).
Library of Congress Cataloging-in-Publication Data is available.

ISBN: 978-1-63528-198-9

All rights reserved. Printed in the United States of America.

Scripture quotations are from New Revised Standard Version Bible, copyright © 1989 National Council of the Churches of Christ in the United States of America. Used by permission. All rights reserved worldwide.

Cover photograph by David Cassady.

Contents

Rationale 1
Introduction 3
Part 1: God's Character Constrains His Actions 21
   Truth 25
   Righteousness 31
   Love 37
Part 2: God's Natural Principles Constrain His Actions 43
   Unity 47
   Consistency 53
   Progression 61
Part 3: God's Gift of Human Freedom Constrains His Actions 67
   Being 71
   Thinking 79
   Doing 85
Conclusion 91

Rationale

No one is immune to tragedy. It's a universal phenomenon. Even though we have been unusually fortunate and enjoy good health, many tragedies have still touched our lives:

In 1952 Maralene's brother, Charles Woolsey, was killed in a freak tractor accident. This bright, happy little boy was only eight years old.

In 1973 our sister-in-law's mother, Ellen Trantham, was fatally injured in an automobile crash. She was a vital, much-loved mother and grandmother.

In 1973 our sister-in-law's brother, Russell McCury, was shot in the line of duty as a law enforcement officer. He was a responsible, young family man.

In 1975 Miles's father, J. Fred Wesner, was diagnosed with terminal cancer. This devout Christian minister suffered unbelievable pain before his death at age eighty in 1978.

In 1979 Miles's mother, Pearl Mae Wesner, had a debilitating stroke that left her paralyzed and speechless. She lived for nine years in frustration, unable to communicate or function independently.

In 1981 our nephew, Colorado Wesner, disappeared while on a neighborhood errand. Weeks later the police found his decomposed body in an abandoned house. This beautiful, delightful child was only five years old.

In January 1984 Maralene's brother, Bobby Woolsey, was killed by a stray bullet when he answered a wrecker call. This talented, dedicated musician was only twenty-six years old, a husband and father.

In September 1984 Maralene's father, Loyse Woolsey, was operating his wrecking service when a speeding car ended his life at age seventy-two. He was a respected businessman, dedicated Christian, and adored father and grandfather.

In 1985 Maralene's mother, Evelyene West, died at age sixty-nine from a chronic lung condition. This brilliant teacher and thinker had lived courageously for many years with great discomfort.

In 1986 our sister-in-law, Nila Wesner, endured two days of intensive surgery to remove a massive brain tumor. The trauma and damage were too severe. She emerged from surgery in severe depression and died by suicide when she was only forty-nine with one son in seminary and one in college.

In 2009, Miles's brother died of leukemia at age seventy-five. He had been an outstanding superintendent of schools and music director in his local church. He was a deacon and taught a Sunday school class until a few months before his death.

In addition to these family experiences, we have spent almost seventy years as religious and educational counselors. We have dealt with literally hundreds of such inexplicable tragedies. We have listened to literally hundreds of confused, angry, disillusioned individuals. We have seen literally hundreds of situations when painful reality absolutely repudiated traditional dogma. Since we were not willing to "cop out" in the face of these incongruities, we began to explore new paths with startling theological implications.

By sharing the insights we've gained from our professional as well as our personal life, we hope to strengthen others who hurt. Indeed, if intellectual enlightenment can be increased, it will lend some meaning to these deaths. If emotional comfort can be extended, then these will not have suffered in vain. If spiritual dimensions can be expanded, we'll see that it is possible for evil things to work together for good. Therefore, it is to these loved ones and the millions of others they represent that this book is dedicated.

Introduction

A newspaper headline reads, "Four Children Die in Home Fire." The article describes how fierce blazes ripped through a mobile home, killing four small children while their mother attended a nearby church.

A young correspondent wrote an honest letter:

Dear God:

Why did you let my little brother die? He was hit by the car, and we prayed for you to let him live, but you didn't. He was only two years old, and he couldn't have sinned bad enough to be punished that way. Everyone says you are good and can do anything you want to do. Then you could have saved my little brother. You let him die and broke my mother's heart. How can I love you?

An article in a Hollywood journal enumerates a star's many misfortunes. "This actress has endured an unbelievable series of tragedies. Her eight-year-old daughter contracted measles and died suddenly. Her eighteen-month-old son was struck by a taxi and crippled for life. Soon thereafter, she herself suffered several debilitating strokes. Her bewildered comment was: 'I think surely God must have blinked.'"

It's evident from these examples and thousands of others that life poses one basic question. Theology agonizes over one basic question.

Philosophy analyzes one basic question. In the depths of our personal despair, we wrestle with one basic question. That momentous, ever-present question is this: "Why does a good God allow evil?"

We confront this painful dilemma when babies die. We confront it when cancer wins. We confront it when catastrophes strike. Every honest, sensitive individual has experienced anguish over these problems: Why do storms destroy indiscriminately? Why are innocent motorists crippled in car wrecks? Why are moral, productive people killed while immoral, unproductive people survive?

These questions must be faced! The obvious unfairness can't be denied. The unpleasant facts can't be ignored. The sense of outrage can't be suppressed. These tragedies occur everywhere. They occur regularly. Many are unjustified and unreasonable. No amount of "fixing" will reconcile the conflicts. No sanctimonious platitudes will satisfy the bereaved. An informed ethical generation rightly rejects the old shallow, traditional cliches.

We've heard "God works in mysterious ways," but Jesus said, "To you it has been given to know the secrets of the kingdom of heaven" (Matt 13:11).

We've heard "we must accept God's will," but Jesus said, "It is not the will of your Father in heaven that one of these little ones should be lost" (Matt 18:14).

We've heard "we're just not meant to know," but Jesus said, "There is nothing hidden, except to be disclosed; nor is anything secret, except to come to light. If you have ears to hear, then hear!" (Mark 4:22–23).

We've heard "we'll understand it better by and by," but Jesus said, "Blessed are your eyes, for they see, and your ears, for they hear" (Matt 13:16).

Solving the painful dichotomy of an all-righteous, all-powerful God is crucial in today's world. To ordinary people the intellectual conflict is this: If God can abolish evil and doesn't, he's not all-righteous! If God wants to abolish evil and can't, he's not all-powerful. That's the dichotomy! In fact, this dichotomy has always existed. Complaints have always been voiced. Questions have always been asked.

Job asked them:

> I loathe my life; I will give free utterance to my complaint; I will speak in the bitterness of my soul.... Although you know that I am not guilty, and there is no one to deliver out of your hand? Your hands fashioned and made me, and now you turn and destroy me. Remember that you fashioned me like clay, and will you turn me to dust again?" (Job 10:1, 7–9)

> I would speak to the Almighty, and I desire to argue my case with God.... Why do you hide your face and count me as your enemy? (Job 13:3, 24)

> Even when I cry out, "Violence!" I am not answered; I call aloud, but there is no justice. (Job 19:7)

> Why do the wicked live on, reach old age, and grow mighty in power? Their children are established in their presence and their offspring before their eyes. Their houses are safe from fear, and no rod of God is upon them. (Job 21:7-9)

> Did I not weep for those whose day was hard? Was not my soul grieved for the poor? But when I looked for good, evil came, and when I waited for light, darkness came. (Job 30:25–26)

The Bible explains that Job was vindicated and rewarded but not enlightened. The questions remained.

David asked them:

> Why, O LORD, do you stand far off? Why do you hide yourself in times of trouble? (Ps 10:1)

> How long, O LORD? Will you forget me forever? How long will you hide your face from me? How long must I bear pain in my soul and have sorrow in my heart all day long? How long shall my enemy be exalted over me? (Ps 13:1–2)

> My God, my God, why have you forsaken me? Why are you so far from helping me, from the words of my groaning? O my God, I cry by day, but you do not answer; and by night but find no rest. (Ps 22:1–2)

David was a great king, a man after God's own heart, but he never understood life's paradoxes. The questions remained.

Many other psalmists asked them:

> For I was envious of the arrogant; I saw the prosperity of the wicked. For they have no pain; their bodies are sound and sleek. They are not in trouble as others are; they are not plagued like other people.... Such are the wicked; always at ease, they increase in riches. All in vain I have kept my heart clean and washed my hands in innocence. For all day long I have been plagued and am punished every morning. (Ps 73:3–5, 12–14)

> But I, O LORD, cry out to you; in the morning my prayer comes before you. O LORD, why do you cast me off? Why do you hide your face from me? Wretched and close to death from my youth up, I suffer your terrors; I am desperate. (Ps 88:13–15)

> O LORD, how long shall the wicked, how long shall the wicked exult? (Ps 94:3)

The psalms endured and gave strength to millions, but the questions remained.

Jeremiah asked them:

> You will be in the right, O LORD, when I lay charges against you, but let me put my case to you. Why does the way of the guilty prosper? Why do all who are treacherous thrive? (Jer 12:1)
>
> Have you completely rejected Judah? Does your heart loathe Zion? Why have you struck us down so that there is no healing for us? We looked for peace but find no good, for a time of healing, but there is terror instead. (Jer 14:19)
>
> Is evil a recompense for good? Yet they have dug a pit for my life. (Jer 18:20)
>
> O LORD, you have enticed me, and I was enticed; you have overpowered me, and you have prevailed. I have become a laughingstock all day long; everyone mocks me. (Jer 20:7)

Jeremiah survived and influenced the world, but the questions remained.

Other prophets asked them:

> O LORD, how long shall I cry for help, and you will not listen? Or cry to you "Violence!" and you will not save? Why do you make me see wrongdoing and look at trouble? Destruction and violence are before me; strife and contention arise. So the law becomes slack, and justice never prevails. The wicked surround the righteous; therefore judgment comes forth perverted. (Hab 1:2–4)

The Jewish prophets shaped civilization and prepared the way for Christianity, but the questions remained.

Even Jesus asked them:

> My God, my God, why have you forsaken me? (Matt 27:46)

Meekly accepting our fate solves no problems. Saying *disease does not exist* never effected a cure for polio. Saying *tornados are acts of God* never developed a storm warning satellite system. Saying *we must deserve this punishment* never alleviated a plague or abolished a war!

On the contrary, all humanitarian accomplishments have come out of belief systems that stubbornly regard evil as an unwelcome interloper in God's universe. If God deliberately sends these evils as punishments, then we shouldn't try to abolish them. If God permissively allows these evils as methods of discipline, then we shouldn't fight them. If God sends illness to punish immorality, then we're working against him when we offer treatment.

This kind of thinking will eventually destroy mankind. In fact, this kind of thinking has already hindered and impeded every step of human progress. For instance, lightning rods were condemned because preachers said, "Lightning is God's weapon against evildoers."

When ether was first used as anesthesia for childbirth, many religious groups protested, saying, "God ordained the suffering of women because Eve ate the forbidden fruit!" If we really believed these deadly doctrines, we'd still be living in caves. No new medical discoveries would be made. No labor-saving techniques would be invented. No pain-alleviating drugs would be developed. If we really believed these deadly doctrines, we'd still have natural life spans of twenty to thirty years!

No! Evil is to be understood. Its causes are to be discovered. Its consequences are to be prevented. Evil is real, but it stands in stark contradiction to a good God!

The problem of evil inevitably leads to the subject of prayer. A wife prays, "God, is it fair for my husband to lose his job?" A woman cries, "Lord, I don't understand why my grandmother has to bear such great pain." A man asks, "Why did all those people lose their lives in that earthquake?" Haven't we all wanted to question God?

Worshipers over the years have not only questioned; they have tried to find answers through the process known as prayer.

If prayer is "the soul's sincere desire, unuttered or expressed," then we must admit that Christianity has no monopoly on it.

Epictetus, a Roman philosopher, said, "When thou has shut thy door and darkened thy room, say not to thyself that thou are alone. God is there."

In the Aztec ruins archaeologists found these words: "O merciful Lord, let this chastisement, with which Thou has visited us, give us freedom from evil and from folly."

The Khands of India chant, "O Lord, we know not what is good for us. Thou knowest what it is. For it we pray."

Xenophon preceded each day's march with prayer.

Pericles began every oration with prayer.

Homer's *Iliad* begins with prayer.

Socrates cried, "I pray Thee, O God, that I might be beautiful within."

Plato said, "Every person of sense, before beginning any important work, will ask help of the gods."

Even in today's world we pray to God like children write letters to Santa Claus. We sanctimoniously intone them at public functions to lend an air of piety. We conscientiously murmur them in personal crises just to be on the safe side.

St. Augustine reminded us that "we may pray most when we say the least; and we may pray the least when we say the most."

Jesus agreed, saying, "[People] think that they will be heard because of their many words" (Matt 6:7).

Yet Paul said, "Pray without ceasing" (1 Thess 5:17).

If both injunctions are valid, then prayer must be more than mere talk.

Victor Hugo said certain thoughts are prayers: "There are moments when, whatever the inclination of the body, the soul is on its knees."

Each person prays best in his or her own way.

Paul knelt in prayer: "When he had finished speaking, he knelt down with them all and prayed" (Acts 20:36).

Jeremiah stood in prayer: "Give heed to me, O LORD.... Remember how I stood before you to speak good for them" (Jer 18:19, 20).

David sat in prayer: "Then King David went in and sat before the LORD, and said, 'Who am I, O Lord GOD, and what is my house, that you have brought me thus far?'" (2 Sam 7:18).

Jesus fell on his face in prayer: "And going a little farther, he threw himself on the ground and prayed, 'My Father, if it is possible, let this cup pass from me, yet not what I want but what you want'" (Matt 26:39).

Hannah prayed silently: "[She] was praying silently; only her lips moved, but her voice was not heard" (1 Sam 1:13).

Ezekiel prayed aloud: "Then I fell down on my face, cried with a loud voice, and said, 'Ah Lord GOD! You are finishing off the remnant of Israel!'" (Ezek 11:13).

Some prayed in temples: "Hezekiah went up to the house of the LORD...and...prayed before the LORD" (2 Kgs 19:14, 15).

The psalmist prayed in bed: "My mouth praises you with joyful lips when I think of you on my bed and meditate on you in the watches of the night" (Ps 63:5–6).

Some prayed in the field; others prayed by the river: "On the Sabbath day we went outside the gate by the river, where we supposed there was a place of prayer, and we sat down and spoke to the women who had gathered there" (Acts 16:13).

Some prayed on battlefields: "Then Samuel said, 'Gather all Israel at Mizpah, and I will pray to the LORD for you.'... As Samuel was offering up the burnt offering, the Philistines drew near to attack Israel" (1 Sam 7:5, 10).

Others pray in quiet rooms: "Whenever you pray, go into your room and shut the door and pray to your Father who is in secret, and your Father who sees in secret will reward you" (Matt 6:6).

With so many different ideas and descriptions regarding prayer, it's understandable that its purposes and practices are often distorted.

Does prayer operate like a royal telephone? Can we simply dial a deity when we choose? Do we, like the movie character E.T., get an urge to "phone home" when loneliness or anxiety depresses us?

The whole subject is relevant and vital. The promise that men and women can converse, fellowship, and agree together with their Creator is one of the most important spiritual developments in the Old Testament. Enoch walked with God. Abraham covenanted with God. Job was a friend of God. The possibilities of this relationship lift human beings into the divine dimension.

From this viewpoint we can begin to see that prayer is not a duty; it's a privilege. We're often told we must read our Bible and pray. We're advised to spend time with our heavenly Father.

Some people even insinuate that the Lord somehow needs our esteem and adoration. That's misleading. Actually, God didn't decree that we should perform this ritual to satisfy him; instead, it's for us! It links us up with divine resources. Too often, we look upon prayer as a holy obligation when the reverse is true: *We* are the ones who benefit.

Regretfully, we don't appreciate anything that is so readily available. Pebbles are not as valuable as diamonds because they are more plentiful, not because they are less useful. Daisies are not as valuable as orchids because they are more common, not because they are less beautiful. We want what we can't have.

Likewise, because the opportunity for prayer is so constant, we don't seek it. Tourists from all over the world make a great effort to see the famous Louvre Museum in Paris, France, while many people who live there have never visited it because they could do so any day.

In St. Peter's Cathedral there is a door that's opened only four times a century. Once every twenty-five years, on Christmas Eve, the pope approaches it in ceremonial attire, with all the cardinals in attendance. He begins the ritual by striking the door three times with a silver hammer. When the passage is opened, the group passes into the cathedral and up the aisle to the altar. The majority of these worshipers have never entered before and will never enter again.

Suppose the way to God's presence was like this "porta sancta" in Rome. Suppose our heavenly Father was inaccessible except once in a quarter of a century. Suppose it has now been ten years since anyone has been permitted to pray. Suppose fifteen years must pass before we can again approach God. Suppose, at most, a person can only hope to offer two or three prayers in a lifetime. If this were the case, we would anticipate and cherish the privilege. Unfortunately, since it is so readily available, we neglect it.

Perhaps we also neglect it because the traditional role of prayer frustrates and confuses us. It raises questions with no answers.

For centuries human beings have sought to discover why tragedies happen. A religious magazine, in surveying the book of Job, commented, "One of the inescapable facts of life is that mankind suffers. Whether religious or not, whether Christian or not, men and women are afflicted by sickness and sorrow."

Why does a God of love and power permit human beings to suffer? Why, in particular, does pain strike the innocent along with the ungodly? These are the theological obstacles upon which the faith of countless individuals has run aground.

Christians can't continue to disregard the discrepancies and avoid the protests. Being forced to face reality is the only way we'll hurt enough to seek answers. Such questions are especially crucial because our own ethical priorities are based upon the ethics of our heavenly Father. Jesus said, "Be perfect, therefore, as your heavenly Father is perfect" (Matt 5:48).

If we're to emulate God, if we're to measure our morals by his standards, if we're to base our behavior on his behavior, if we're to be like him, then we must be sure that our concept of God is true and righteous. If God utterly destroys cities, then massacres are acceptable. If he viciously punishes transgressors, then cruelty and torture are legitimate responses to crime. If he arbitrarily favors some groups over others, then we're free to practice discrimination.

To sidestep these issues is to evade our responsibility in the realm of eternal values. It is to deliberately diminish our light in a dark age.

It is to season with unsavory salt. It is to leaven with inactive yeast. If Christians—supported by God's grace, guided by Jesus's love, and strengthened by the Holy Spirit's power—can't deal with difficult issues, who can?

A preacher commenting on the situation said, "This question is asked by everyone sooner or later. It was the first question asked of me as a minister, and I didn't know how to handle it. As a student pastor I faced a funeral for a nine-year-old boy who had been killed in a bicycle accident. Standing over that casket, his widowed mother asked again and again, 'Why, preacher? Why?'"

It's the first question most ministers are asked, and it will probably be the last question they're asked. It's the most relevant question of life. We've all stood beside patients with needles in their arms, crying out in pain. We've all heard sons and daughters tearfully plead, "Why must she suffer so? Why doesn't God just take her?" It's the first question and the last question of mankind. It's the continuous question and the ageless question.

We are not going to be able to duck this problem. It won't go away! We can hide our heads in the sands of orthodoxy, but when we come up for air, it will still be there! It is persistent! It mocks us, dares us, and forces us into seemingly indefensible positions! In trying to explain it, we fall into insidious moral traps. A devout Christian is killed, and we say, "God took him because he was saved and therefore ready." Then an obvious reprobate is killed, and we say, "God took him because he was evil." These rationalizations are irreconcilable.

A tavern burns down, and we say, "It's the judgment of God." Then a church burns down! One child survives a terrible accident, and we say, "Praise the Lord! He worked a miracle." Then another equally innocent child is painfully mutilated, and there is no miracle. Christians have been eating their words and refusing to acknowledge that their explanations are illogical for centuries.

A religious paper carried the story "Deaths of Missionaries Cause Many to Ask 'Why?'" It described a mission board's records, showing that numerous men and women have been drowned, murdered, killed in car accidents or airplane crashes while serving as missionaries.

Answering the whys of the untimely and seemingly unjust deaths of people dedicated to bringing others to Christ is never easy. It's even harder because certain biblical promises seem to assure us of divine protection. Taking "comforting verses" out of context can set us up for disillusionment.

Proverbs 12:21 reads, "No harm happens to the righteous, but the wicked are filled with trouble." Does this mean that if evil happens to us, we're not righteous?

Psalm 34:7 reads, "The angel of the LORD encamps around those who fear him and delivers them." Where were the angels when our POWs were being tortured in Vietnam and martyrs were being burned at the stake?

Psalm 50:15 reads, "Call on me in the day of trouble; I will deliver you, and you shall glorify me." This must sound hollow to persecuted Christians around the world.

Psalm 91:7, 10–11 reads, "A thousand may fall at your side, ten thousand at your right hand, but it will not come near you.… No evil shall befall you, no scourge come near your tent. For he will command his angels concerning you to guard you in all your ways." Does this mean Christians have absolute protection from diseases?

Jeremiah 1:19 reads, "'They will fight against you, but they shall not prevail against you, for I am with you,' says the Lord, 'to deliver you.'" If this is true, how do we explain the fall of so many countries to the Nazis?

These are life's most perplexing questions, so it's natural for those in dire straits to ask, "Where is God's divine protection?" In the Old Testament, why was Cain spared and Abel killed? Abel would have obviously been a much more productive inhabitant of the earth.

In the New Testament, why was Peter delivered and Stephen stoned? Peter's deliverance is credited to the fact that the church prayed for him! Didn't anyone pray for Stephen?

Analyzing the situation leads to one inevitable conclusion, but that inevitable conclusion is unthinkable! Namely, if God is truly in charge of earthly events, then he's either unfeeling or inefficient! If God causes disasters, pain, and death, he's callous and undeserving of our respect. If, on the other hand, God cannot prevent disasters, pain, and death, he is weak and unworthy of our trust.

What a choice: a cruel God or an incompetent God. This results in both a theological and an emotional impasse.

The reluctance of Christians to relinquish their belief in a God who is both loving and omnipotent has perpetuated this particular dilemma through the centuries. We rightly perceive that if God can't supernaturally protect us in every emergency, then we are relatively alone in the universe! We are vulnerable to nature. We are susceptible to accidents. In short, we are on our own!

Entertaining such a thought is so frightening that most people immediately retreat into the more reassuring though illogical stance known as "blind faith." They prefer a comfortable illusion to a disconcerting truth. It is indeed a disconcerting moment when we realize for the first time that God can't fix everything.

A small child expects mommy to fix bumps and daddy to fix bikes. During his first few years he assumes, therefore, that these larger-than-life authority figures can fix everything. When, as a hurting adolescent, the boy or girl discovers that there are things mom and dad can't fix, a leap into maturity occurs. Hopefully this helps lay the foundation for their own autonomous character.

Likewise, every developing Christian at some point experiences that moment of shock and fear when God doesn't answer. The next step, therefore, invariably involves prayer. If God can't fix things, then what good is prayer? This is a legitimate question.

A news story reported that a three-month-old died in his home after his parents refused medical treatment for him because of religious convictions. The child had been sick for about two weeks but had not received any medical attention. His parents had called on several elders from their church to pray for him.

The district attorney said it would be difficult to file criminal charges because the current law says a parent can depend on prayer to heal a child.

These parents believed very sincerely. These parents had a lot of faith. Yet the child died! They based their decision on Jesus's own words when he said, "Whatever you ask for in prayer with faith, you will receive" (Matt 21:22).

In another case, a young boy died of peritonitis as a result of appendicitis. His parents were charged with manslaughter but acquitted. The state supreme court upheld the acquittal on the grounds that the parents were relying upon the tenets of their religion for the care and protection of their children.

All these people prayed and laid their faith on the line with their lives. What happened? Why didn't God answer? The scripture says, "Whatever you ask for in prayer, believe that you have received it, and it will be yours" (Mark 11:24).

You can see clearly from these examples that it's legitimate to ask, "What good is prayer?" There are deeper levels to be explored. We have to admit that the "prayers" of primitive groups and immature individuals can be useless. Sometimes they are worse than useless. They are actually destructive because they condition the worshipers to apathy. They condition the worshipers to a lack of self-reliance. They condition the worshipers to expect a supernatural "bailout." This sets them up for disillusionment when things don't work out.

Many doctrines about God and prayer lead to superstition. One minister advised viewers of his television program to send in for packets of anointing oil. He said, "Send for these packets and tell me where you hurt. When I pray for you, you may anoint yourself by placing a drop on the affected area of your body. God always responds to prayers made in that manner."

We are rightly skeptical about these claims. Yet the scriptures say, "Are any among you sick? They should call for the elders of the church and have them pray over them, anointing them with oil in the name of the Lord. The prayer of faith will save the sick" (Jas 5:14–15).

Such rituals and practices are so incongruent with modern medical and surgical procedures that even many conservative religious groups condemn these "faith healers." But sanctimoniously claiming "If the Bible says it, I believe it" is hypocritical if you don't really believe it. Indeed, so much confusion abounds that a redefinition of the traditional concept of prayer is essential for modern Christians.

Religion is extremely susceptible to nonsense. We're supposed to be enlightened! We're supposed to be educated! Incidents such as this show that while we may be technologically advanced, we're spiritually retarded. In areas of religion, reason and logic are often ignored. This is a dangerous habit, because if you mistreat your reasoning faculties, you'll lose them. Every time you fix facts or twist truth, you destroy a little bit of your integrity.

It's strange that something so important is so misunderstood. We know very little about prayer. Has it been researched? Have objective scientific studies been made? Have we analyzed the attitudes and practices of productive Christians? Of course not! The whole subject has been declared "off limits" as far as rational, pragmatic discussions are concerned. Examples of this inability to deal with reality are rampant.

In dealing with these issues, many ask questions, but no one ever answers! One woman relates her youthful agonies, saying, "When I was ten years old, I said, 'I don't think God is very nice! How can I love God if I don't like him?' I remember asking: 'Why did God make the Israelites kill all the Canaanites, Grandma? Why did he make them kill the mothers and babies? Babies aren't bad.' They told me I ought to be ashamed to talk like that."

Sometimes children dare to express what adults have learned to suppress. Before we can resolve a dilemma, we must acknowledge its existence. Therefore, someone, sometime, somewhere must analyze reality, discuss incongruities, and make hard decisions concerning God and God's role in earthly events. If we are willing to do this, both our faith and our reason can remain intact.

These questions are profound and complex. Perhaps a hypothetical scenario will clarify some ambiguities. Let's assume that, in the beginning, as the divine "alpha and omega," God was in one sense absolutely omnipotent, able to make any and all choices. However, it's axiomatic that once he defined his character as true, righteous, and loving, his options became limited to some degree. He could no longer exemplify any characteristics or instigate any actions that would be incompatible with these attributes. False, evil, or hateful options were no longer available to him. The scripture says, "God… never lies" (Titus 1:2).

Furthermore, once God established that his natural principles must be unified, consistent, and progressive, his options became more limited. He could no longer operate in ways that would be divisive, inconsistent, or destructive. The scripture says, "I the LORD do not change" (Mal 3:6). Additionally, "every perfect gift is from above, coming down from the Father of lights, with whom there is no variation or shadow due to change" (Jas 1:17).

Finally, once he created human beings and determined their status as free moral agents, his options became even more limited. He could no longer compel attitudes, force insights, or override choices. In short, he can't make individuals be, think, or do anything without their personal consent. Jesus said, "Jerusalem, Jerusalem…how often I desired to gather your children together as a hen gathers her brood under her wings, and you were not willing!" (Luke 13:34).

All of these represent divine limitations. All of these place constraints upon God's actions in this world. All of these have a direct bearing upon the kind of answers we can expect to our prayers.

Those who honestly consider the situation realize that even God can't "have his cake and eat it too." He can't be both righteous and unrighteous. He can't have both a consistent and an inconsistent universe. He can't maintain absolute divine sovereignty and offer absolute freedom to humanity at the same time.

The question then becomes not "Why doesn't God answer?" but rather "How can God answer without contradicting his true, righteous, and loving nature? How can God answer without interfering with his unified, consistent, and progressive universe? How can God answer without nullifying people's personal freedom to be, to think, and to do?"

When our expectations and requests are compatible with these criteria, then our prayers can be answered. When our character becomes true, righteous, and loving, like God's, then our prayers can be answered. Jesus said, "We know that God does not listen to sinners, but he does listen to one who worships him and obeys his will" (John 9:31).

When our desires take into account God's unified, consistent, and progressive natural principles, then our prayers can be answered. Jesus said, "If you abide in me and my words abide in you, ask for whatever you wish, and it will be done for you" (John 15:7).

When our will provides an open channel through which God can work, then our prayers can be answered. John said, "This is the boldness we have in him, that if we ask anything according to his will, he hears us" (1 John 5:14).

Part 1

God's Character Constrains His Actions

Before we can determine what hinders prayer, we must analyze the concept of prayer in light of God's character.

People say, "Let's just pray about it." Christians say, "Pray for me. I'll pray for you." Churches have all-night prayer meetings, and students have prayer partners. There are public prayers and private prayers. There are beautiful written prayers and desperate, spur-of-the-moment prayers. Indeed, prayer is one of the oldest religious rituals. When people find themselves alone in threatening surroundings, they always reach out for something beyond. Just as a baby cries when it is hungry, cold, or afraid, so do men and women instinctively call out in the universal language of petition.

This basic urge to survive and improve is good. This basic motivation to seek understanding and support is good. Shallow applications, however, can lead to superstition. Many Christians need to rethink what they are saying or claiming when they discuss these matters. The validity of prayer is not to prove there is a God. The validity of prayer is not to vindicate God. The validity of prayer is certainly not to demonstrate our own proficiency in influencing God. The first-century Pharisees are not the only arrogant individuals who have turned their prayer sessions into bragging sessions (see Luke 18:10–12).

Some definitions of prayer seem to propagate the ridiculous notion that we have to persuade God to do something he doesn't want to do. Some definitions of prayer seem to insinuate that if we voice our desires eloquently, then God will respond. Some definitions of prayer seem to indicate that if we can only get enough people to beg long enough and hard enough, this combined effort will change God's mind or affect his actions.

Our theology seems to be based on the assumption that spiritual processes operate like civic processes. For example, if enough citizens write or call their congressman, they can influence his decisions. Therefore, perhaps if enough determined Christians bombard heaven with their pleas, they can influence divine purposes.

That's not biblical. Jesus said, "It is your Father's good pleasure to give you the kingdom" (Luke 12:32). If this is true, then there must be other explanations to support the efficacy of prayer.

If God loves us, if he wants the best for us, if he desires to give good gifts, then we know he never deliberately withholds things from us that he is free to give. Jesus explains this, saying, "Is there anyone among you who, if your child asked for bread, would give a stone? Or if the child asked for a fish, would give a snake? If you, then, who are evil, know how to give good gifts to your children, how much more will your Father in heaven give good things to those who ask him!" (Matt 7:9–11).

This promise gives important clues as to the proper role of prayer. Prayer is not a sanctimonious form of appeasement. It is not spiritual bribery. Prayer is not a token that actuates a divine slot machine. Prayer is not a code phrase, like "Open Sesame," that somehow triggers the door to the room where blessings are stashed. Our petitions do not persuade God, and our intercessions do not motivate God.

Rather, prayer is spiritual planning. It illuminates our vision and clears away distractions. The praying person is in tune with life. If God is impartial and just, we must believe he sends divine guidance and insight to everyone. However, it's only those individuals who hear and see and apply these spiritual impulses that benefit. Prayer gets us into an attitude of receptivity. We are then able to hear, remember, think, and understand.

Prayer must take into account the character of God. If we believe this intimate, personal power exists; if we believe he is like Jesus; if we believe he exemplifies complete truth, absolute righteousness, and total love; then we must believe his methods and purposes are in our best interest. It is our own life that is improved when we conform our will to his will, even though all of our requests can't be granted.

It's paradoxical that the very attributes we revere in God—truth, righteousness, and love—can actually be the attributes that constrain his actions.

Truth

The frail little woman was lying on a hospital stretcher when her pastor walked into the emergency room. As they waited for the results of her X-rays, she gripped his hand and cried in desperation, "Please, Pastor, pray that my leg won't be broken. I just can't bear another fracture. I can't handle a heavy cast!"

It was true that she had endured a lot. Her tiny frame was twisted with arthritis. Her bones were brittle with osteomyelitis. For several years she had been almost confined to a wheelchair. The fall that produced this injury had occurred as she tried to reach her bed.

The pastor looked from the hip to the ankle. The alignment was distorted. The knee was turned at an odd angle. A knot protruded almost through the transparent skin. Even as he looked, the pitiful old voice quavered. "Pray! Please, Brother, pray that my leg won't be broken!"

This kind of scenario is played out daily in every city of the world. The characters and circumstances vary, but the question is the same. Over and over again, Christians are confronted with similar heart-rending situations.

What should this minister do in such a case? The leg was broken. The fact was obvious. The complications would be clearly revealed on the X-ray within minutes. How could he respond to her plea? If he prayed for it to show no fracture, he'd be a hypocrite, setting her up for future disillusionment. If he refused to pray as she requested, she'd have a right to say, "Then you don't believe in prayer! What good is a God who can't help us in emergencies?"

If the preacher did what the majority of us do in these cases, he probably evaded the issue and prayed for nebulous "spiritual" things like "courage, faith, and strength." Worse yet, he might have copped out by mouthing one of two pious phrases: "If you will just believe enough" or "If it's the Lord's will." These no-risk approaches reveal spiritual cowardice. It lets either the victim or the Lord take the rap for the seriousness of the injury and the pain that ensues.

Now, none of these responses is adequate. We know it is not God's will for anyone to suffer. His perfect will is that every person be well, whole, and happy. Jesus, when he was acting on earth for the heavenly Father, never left any seeking soul hurting. In every encounter it always seemed to be the "Lord's will" for healing to take place. When this woman pleaded, "Pray that my leg won't be broken," she deserved an honest reply. Furthermore, she and other Christians like her deserve better teachings, better explanations, and better theology.

Now, concerning prayer: Why couldn't that particular petition be answered? What assumption was it based upon? What methods would it have required? What precedent would it have set? These are hard questions.

In answering them, the first criteria we must examine is God himself. It's absolutely axiomatic that his character constrains his actions. Jesus said, "Good trees bring forth good fruit." Grapes produce grapes, figs produce figs, and thistles produce thistles (see Matt 7:16–20). In other words, what a thing is determines what it does, and what it does proves what it is! Therefore, it is imperative that God exemplifies truth. If he is indeed a God of truth, then his methods and responses must verify this fact.

Truth encompasses reality, reliability, and reason. God must be true to himself. Many people say, "Oh, God can do anything!" No, he can't! There are many things his nature won't permit him to do. He cannot do things that will thwart his overall purposes. This idea is emphasized before the destruction of Sodom, when God said to Lot, "Hurry, escape there, for I can do nothing until you arrive there" (Gen 19:22).

Also, God cannot undo, revise, or reverse processes. The scriptures say, "God is not a human being, that he should lie, or a mortal, that he should change his mind. Has he promised, and will he not do it? Has he spoken, and will he not fulfill it? See, I received a command to bless; he has blessed, and I cannot revoke it" (Num 23:19–20).

The fact that God cannot lie doesn't merely mean he has to eschew false statements. It doesn't merely mean he has to avoid careless promises. It doesn't merely mean he has to present correct information. It goes much deeper. It means his character must be consistent. The essence of his being must contain no conflicts, no incongruities, and no contradictions. God is! The "I AM WHO I AM" spoken to Moses expresses well the concept of a God who embodies universal realities (see Exod 3:14).

Truth is an indivisible, cohesive unit. It can't be added to or subtracted from. The phrase "the whole truth and nothing but the truth" is actually redundant since truth by its very nature is whole and complete. It lacks nothing. Truth incorporates all the facts, principles, and applications that govern life.

This attribute of God is emphasized in Scripture: "'I am the Alpha and the Omega,' says the Lord God, 'who is and who was and who is to come, the Almighty'" (Rev 1:8). God isn't just a strong creature occupying a throne somewhere in the heavens. He is the all-encompassing force—the instigator, the energizer, and the culminator of life. He is the dynamics of the universe!

The phrase "the whole truth and nothing but the truth" is also redundant because truth by its very nature includes no extraneous or deceptive material. This attribute of God is emphasized in the following scripture: "I will proclaim the name of the LORD, ascribe greatness to our God! The Rock, his work is perfect, and all his ways are just. A faithful God, without deceit, just and upright is he" (Deut 32:3–4).

God's works, deeds, and methods are perfect. The word *perfect* means "whole and complete." Nothing is lacking. His ways and his modes of action are just. This means operating according to divine law. He's a God of truth. His word means stable, steady, and established. His character contains no iniquity, distorted morals, or unjust verdicts.

Truth by its very nature is permanent. Therefore, it can never be more or less than absolute. The writer of Ecclesiastes was able to perceive this divine characteristic, saying, "I know that whatever God does endures forever; nothing can be added to it nor anything taken from it.... That which is already has been; that which is to be already is, and God seeks out what has gone by" (Eccl 3:14–15).

This insight should modify our immature concepts of a God who created and then repents of his actions, of a God who comes down to inspect the earth and then changes the course of history, of a God who arbitrarily extends and then withdraws protection. These are destructive and invalid descriptions of God. He is immutable.

Now, what does the knowledge that God exemplifies truth have to do with our concepts of prayer? The main thing it does is force us to look deeper into our requests. We must analyze our desires and expectations to see if they are based on false assumptions. We must analyze our desires and expectations to see if they would require invalid actions. We must analyze our desires and expectations to see if their fulfillment would lead to fundamental incongruities.

If our requests are based on false assumptions, they will collapse like houses built on the sand. If our requests require invalid acts or take unfair advantages, then they are inherently immoral and cannot have divine sanction. If our requests would lead to fundamental incongruities and cause future chaos in the universe, then they must be reconsidered and redefined. We should know in advance that such desires could not be fulfilled. Such expectations could not be realized. Such prayers could not be answered.

The principle that God is truth takes precedence over any personal aspirations or social achievements. God cannot grant petitions that would reward false premises. God cannot grant petitions that would validate deceitful methods. God cannot grant petitions that would set up destructive processes.

Sincere delusions about a magical God can't be sustained. Sooner or later, the reality of life will assert itself, and that person who lives in a dream world will find himself in a nightmare. The person who bases his actions on a religious fantasy will find himself caught in a fatal trap! Disillusionment, bitterness, and actual physical harm can result.

Jesus was choosing scientific reality over traditional promises when he refused to jump from the pinnacle of the temple. Cults that practice snake-handling and the drinking of poison don't demonstrate God's power. They demonstrate their own ignorance. Preachers who drive ninety miles an hour because they foolishly believe they lead a charmed life don't demonstrate God's power. They demonstrate their own stupidity.

Deception—even a pleasant, desirable, and soothing deception—eventually enslaves. But truth—even an unpleasant, undesirable, and frightening truth—eventually liberates! Jesus said, "You will know the truth, and the truth will make you free" (John 8:32).

Truth is one of the divine attributes Jesus emphasized and manifested. He placed it as the cornerstone of his ministry, saying, "I am the way and the truth and the life" (John 14:6). You cannot reach God in any other way. You cannot gain access to spiritual power in any other way. You cannot even approach eternal dimensions in any other way. The way of life is the way of truth.

Now, this woman's prayer concerning her leg could not be answered because the truth cannot be denied. There is an inexorable law of cause and effect that had already been fulfilled. There are reliable principles involving gravity, stress, and pressure; these principles cannot be nullified. Certain processes had occurred; they could not be reversed. Certain facts existed; they could not be eradicated.

Truth is a powerful thing. It's been greatly underestimated by everyone from the serpent in the garden of Eden to politicians in Washington, D.C. It was potent in the dawn of creation, and it is potent in the twenty-first century. The psalmist said, "For the LORD is good; his steadfast love endures forever and his faithfulness to all generations" (Ps 100:5).

No one can ignore truth and live. Don't sell it short! It must permeate our entire being. Jesus said, "Sanctify them in the truth; your word is truth" (John 17:17).

Our perception of truth determines our success in life. Delusions, illusions, and deceptions will fail, but truth will stand. We as Christians have inside information on this subject. We have an ally in this department. We have direct access to the essence of things. Let's take advantage of it. Jesus said, "When the Spirit of truth comes, he will guide you into all the truth" (John 16:13).

Truth seekers don't seek one exclusive point of view. They seek all possible points of view. Truth is what's there, not necessarily what you've been told! Truth is what's there, not just what you can see at the moment! Planets yet undiscovered are still there. Mountaintops hidden by clouds are still there. The sins and flaws we deny are still there.

Base your life, your actions, and your prayers upon truth.

Righteousness

The huge airliner with hundreds of passengers aboard crashed in a storm. Such a disaster is expected to occur occasionally in a rapidly moving technological society. Almost all the travelers were killed, some from massive head wounds and internal injuries and others from the smoke and fire that followed the impact. Miraculously, three people escaped almost untouched. In the midst of death, one of the fortunate survivors exclaimed reverently, "Man, the Lord was surely looking after me today!"

Now, what's wrong with that statement? Most Christians would say, "There's nothing wrong with it! He is showing a humble spirit! He is expressing a proper sense of gratitude! He is acknowledging and praising God!"

On the surface it sounds so good. Beneath the surface, however, several destructive premises are being voiced: If God's hand was specifically on the survivors, why wasn't his hand on those who died? How does the belief that God delivered the few make the relatives of all the others feel? Those families must ask, "Why wasn't my son or daughter or husband or wife or mother or father as important as those three? Why did God desert them in their hour of need? Were they evil? Did they do something to cause this? Is my family unworthy?"

Great guilt, resentment, conflict, and bitterness result from such experiences. The implications involved when God seems to protect some and neglect others are subtle. They aren't always voiced, but they are there!

How would you feel if a lifeguard saved several kids from a shark attack and callously allowed your child to be killed? That's exactly how you would feel toward God in such cases, whether you are willing to admit it or not! The feelings may be denied or suppressed, but they are there, and they are deadly!

Among those who perished in this particular accident were two missionary doctors, greatly needed in their places of service. There were young mothers, now separated from their children. There were rich playboys bound for a gambling resort, obviously unprepared for eternity. There were also innocent babies and honest businessmen.

If we claim that God's hand reached down in some supernatural way to personally pick out two or three individuals for life, then we are also claiming that he personally consigned the others to death. At this point in a discussion, most people begin to feel quite uncomfortable. They say, "Well, the good Lord must have had his reasons!" or "It's just not right for us to question such things!"

This clearly shows that we are theological cowards. We will accept immoral religious explanations without protest if this is the only way we can retain our selfish, immature security blanket! We actually prefer an unfair God to one who may not be able to deliver us from a crisis situation.

When that plane was plunging to the ground, it's almost certain that many of those who were killed had prayed, "Oh, God, save us!" Why weren't their prayers answered? Is it reasonable to assume that none of those doomed people had any further purpose in life? Is it reasonable to assume that the three who survived are the only ones who would have done anything worthwhile in the years to come? Is it reasonable to assume that there were mysterious justifications to explain why the hundreds of others perished?

Did God really single them out and protect them in some special way? Did he literally hold them in his hand? Did he throw divine armor around them? Did he suspend natural laws in their case? Did he move them out of danger like so many chess pieces?

We need to know what we are claiming and realize what we are suggesting when we make religious statements. To glorify God means to make him look good! This doctrine doesn't do that! Also, consider Jesus's life. He is the best picture of God that we have. If Jesus wouldn't do it, then God wouldn't do it!

Intellectuals and agnostics who ridicule illogical religious claims deserve a straightforward answer. These are vital issues that must be dealt with in today's world. It's better not to believe in any God than to believe in a false one! A faulty God, like a faulty parachute, is worse than none at all, since you will be depending on that concept in an emergency.

In order to achieve any measure of credibility, we must look at God himself and remember that his character constrains his actions. God must exemplify righteousness. The scripture says, "His work is perfect, and all his ways are just. A faithful God, without deceit, just and upright is he" (Deut 32:4).

The attribute of righteousness encompasses honesty, justice, and virtue. That which is righteous is worthy of honor. That which is righteous deserves respect. That which is righteous is fair, legitimate, and moral. The psalmist said, "He is coming to judge the earth. He will judge the world with righteousness and the peoples with his truth" (Ps 96:13).

The righteousness of God is proclaimed hundreds of times in the scriptures from Genesis to Revelation. The righteousness of God is the underlying theme of both the Old and New Testaments. The righteousness of God is stressed so constantly because everything depends upon it!

An unrighteous, immoral, unfair God is reprehensible. An unrighteous, immoral, unfair God undermines the entire system of existence. Indeed, nothing else matters if the creator, the energizer, and the supreme model of our universe deviates from a position of unqualified moral integrity.

Without a righteous deity, life has no meaning. Without a righteous deity, action has no purpose. Without a righteous deity, the future has no hope. Without goal posts, even a football game is an exercise in futility. Without a finish line, a race represents a senseless waste of energy. Without a foundation, a building is a dangerous sham. People must have something they can depend on. They must have something to emulate. They must have something to reach for. Individuals must have an ideal by which they can evaluate their behavior.

Society will never advance beyond the ethical level of their idea of God. If we believe in a God who can act arbitrarily and unfairly, then we will feel justified in doing so. If we believe in a God who retaliates and avenges, then we will feel justified in doing so.

Our attitudes and reactions are definitely determined by our concept of God. Cultures that worship a vengeful deity are vengeful and violent. The moral standard of the universe, of civilization, and of humanity is based upon God's righteous character. Peter said, "It is written, 'You shall be holy, for I am holy'" (1 Pet 1:16).

How does recognizing the fact that God exemplifies righteousness affect our prayer expectations? In the first place, it eliminates certain expectations and gives strict guidelines for the others. A righteous God can't pick and choose who he will aid and who he will refuse to aid. A righteous God can't concoct a miracle just because one person begs a little more earnestly than another. A righteous God can't show partiality to a certain individual simply because he performs a few more religious rituals than another. Peter said, "I truly understand that God shows no partiality, but in every people anyone who fears him and practices righteousness is acceptable to him" (Acts 10:34–35).

A righteous God can't be bribed with sacrifices and offerings. A righteous God can't be swayed by promises and prayers! The scripture says, "The LORD your God is God of gods and Lord of lords, the great God, mighty and awesome, who is not partial and takes no bribe" (Deut 10:17).

Instead of expecting special treatment or miraculous intervention, we should try to understand the overall plan of the universe. We should analyze long-term processes. We should consider actions and their consequences. As Christians we should always ask, "What if God did this for everyone?" If the result would be negative, then he can't do it for me!

In a world of moral order, the consequences of actions have to be linked inexorably to the value of those actions. Good trees must produce good fruit, and bad trees must produce bad fruit. Good fountains must have good water, and bad fountains must have bad water. There would be chaos instead of order if grapevines produced thistles and thorn trees produced figs. The system wouldn't work! The whole structure of the universe would break down within minutes if evil was rewarded and good was punished. Paul said, "There will be affliction and distress for everyone who does evil, both the Jew first and the Greek, but glory and honor and peace for everyone who does good, both the Jew first and the Greek. For God shows no partiality" (Rom 2:9–11).

The truth of a concept is tested by its success in life. If a mixture blows up in the laboratory, we say, "Evidently that was wrong!" Life doesn't lie, and neither does God.

For man to truly reap what he sows (see Gal 6:7), a dependable policy of cause and effect has to be in operation. For this policy to work, there cannot be any exceptions. Nature, life, and Scripture all agree that no amount of pleading can change the boomerang effect of a destructive deed once the negative process has been set into motion. Paul said, "The wrongdoer will be paid back for whatever wrong has been done, and there is no partiality" (Col 3:25).

These unfortunate results are not retribution or punishments. God does forgive, so we need not endure guilt, but we must endure the natural consequences of our actions.

Now, what do these concepts concerning God's righteous character have to do with prayer and tragedy? Both spiritual knowledge and common sense tell us that airplanes do not crash because God gets angry. Airplanes do not crash because people neglect prayer. Airplanes crash because laws are broken! You may call them natural laws or scientific laws, but they are, nonetheless, God's laws! The same God who decreed the principle of love decreed the principle of gravity.

Jesus said, "It is easier for heaven and earth to pass away than for one stroke of a letter in the law to be dropped" (Luke 16:17).

Even Jesus's parables would be invalid if some laws are natural and operate in one way and others are "supra-natural" and operate in a different way. You can't break any of God's laws with impunity. The people who died in the plane crash were not being punished by God. They were simply experiencing the awful consequences of a broken law. They were in the wrong place at the wrong time. They were suffering the effects of someone's negligence or ignorance.

As part of the human family, we all pay the price for the mistakes and sins of others. The innocent and the guilty are often together in a tragedy. Our prayers, in such cases, must include requests for knowledge and dedication to duty. The engineers and the mechanics have to be dependable. The pilots and the weather forecasters have to be prepared. People are responsible for most accidents. When lightning or natural forces cause the problems, then our prayers have to be directed toward scientists and technicians who will be able to discover ways of predicting, controlling, or mitigating the results of dangerous situations. God won't adjust cosmic laws to meet our specifications.

The person who lives with this expectation wastes his life. We never look at an unplanted field and ask for corn. We never mix flour and water and say, "Make my bread rise without yeast." Now, God does make corn grow and bread rise, but only if the human agent has followed the rules. Therefore, we must learn how the universe works so we can intelligently adjust ourselves to it since it certainly won't adjust itself to us!

Our speculations should not be about *if* God answers prayer, but rather about *how* God answers prayer.

Love

The little girl was a model student. She was bright, sensitive, loving, and full of promise. Her mind held that unusual balance of inquisitive curiosity and disciplined determination. Her potential was unlimited. Full of the zest of life, she played as hard as she worked.

One day on the school playground, she slipped on an old merry-go-round and cut her foot. It was a nasty gash, but she took it in stride, coming to class on crutches so as not to miss one day from her exciting studies.

Unfortunately, the injury didn't heal as rapidly as her parents had hoped. They applied the usual home remedies and finally took her to a local doctor. He dressed it but also noticed something else. She seemed to have a slight case of mumps. Sore jaws caused pain when she ate. Everyone said, "Never mind; there's nothing to worry about!"

Days went by, and her condition worsened. By the time a correct diagnosis was made in a larger hospital, it was too late! The tetanus was too far advanced. Neither modern medicine, breathing machines, nor a church prayer chain could save her. She died! A brilliant mind, a lovely personality, a great future snuffed out at the age of ten.

Was this God's will? Was it his "intentional will," as a few misguided individuals insinuated? In other words, did an omnipotent power push her foot onto a sharp metal bar? Were the deadly tetanus germs placed in that exact spot by divine decree? Did God cause these parents to delay making a doctor's appointment? Did he deliberately force the physicians to make a wrong diagnosis? Did he personally intervene so the medicines and machines would not work?

"Oh, no!" people in this more enlightened age protest. "Of course God didn't do those things. It wasn't his intentional will; it was his permissive will."

What's that?

"Oh, he didn't cause it to happen; he merely permitted it to happen. He didn't create the deadly set of circumstances; he merely decided that in this particular situation he would allow it to occur."

It may be very upsetting for those who use this explanation to learn that there's no difference! If God can do something positive and doesn't do it, he's just as liable as if he did something negative.

Suppose there is a hospital ward full of patients dying from a rare poison and you have the antidote. If you arbitrarily choose to administer this medicine to a few patients and allow the others to die in agony, you are as guilty of their deaths as if you had poisoned them! Knowing how to do good, or having the ability to do good and not doing it, is just as sinful as it is to deliberately do evil. James said, "Anyone, then, who knows the right thing to do and fails to do it commits sin" (Jas 4:17). We can't fall back on such lame doctrines any longer!

Then why did this child die? Was God asleep? Was he negligent? Did he ignore the numerous intercessions made in her behalf? Did he say, "Sorry, but that's just not the request I've decided to answer today"?

Perhaps there weren't enough petitions. How many more would it have taken to save her? Would one more impassioned entreaty have turned the tide? Would a better-worded plea have moved God to act? That's ridiculous!

Once more, we must look at God himself since his character constrains his actions.

God must exemplify love: "Whoever does not love does not know God, for God is love…. God is love, and those who abide in love abide in God. and God abides in them" (1 John 4:8, 16).

This scripture, and hundreds more like it, assures us that God cannot do things that would bring harm to anyone. Love rules out revenge, retaliation, and hatred. Instead, love includes affection, good will, and respect for others. If God is total love, then his affection, good will, and respect for us are total.

This insight clarifies certain doctrines. Forgiveness, for instance, can't be something that is triggered in God's heart by our act of repentance. Instead, his forgiveness is there all the time. Repentance simply opens our own heart to the realization of that forgiveness.

Furthermore, vengeance is ruled out of the eternal scenario. A loving God could not impose a penalty that is not redemptive. Suffering that teaches, motivates, or shapes character can be tolerated within a universal moral system, but suffering that is imposed with no purpose, intent, or hope of alleviation cannot be attributed to God.

If God's love is unconditional, then it doesn't depend upon the recipient's character, behavior, or response. Paul said, "God proves his love for us in that while we still were sinners Christ died for us" (Rom 5:8).

If God's love is eternal, then it doesn't vary. It can't be increased, diminished, or terminated. The scripture says, "The LORD appeared to him from far away. 'I have loved you with an everlasting love; therefore I have continued my faithfulness to you'" (Jer 31:3).

Now, what does the fact that God exemplifies love have to do with our prayer practices? For one thing, it helps us rise above immature requests: "Samson called to the LORD and said, 'Lord GOD, remember me and strengthen me only this once, O God, so that with this one act of revenge I may pay back the Philistines for my two eyes'" (Judg 16:28). Centuries later, Stephen, dying from the stones of his tormentors, prayed, "Lord, do not hold this sin against them!" (Acts 7:60). Both were prayers, but they were eons apart ethically. One demands revenge, the other extends forgiveness. Which one is compatible with a God of love?

In the final analysis, "He prayest best who lovest best." Through prayer we try to find and align ourselves with God's purposes. John said, "If we ask anything according to his will, he hears us" (1 John 5:14).

When our individual will is at odds with the divine will, ours must be subordinated, not for his benefit, but for ours. A pagan voiced this wise petition, saying, "Grant us the good whether we pray for it or not, but keep the evil from us even though we pray for it." He is saying, "God, see beneath my shallow words. Give me what I truly need even though I may ask for a superficial or dangerous substitute."

God, the universe, and life do this automatically if we abide by natural laws and live by constructive principles. "What we sow, we reap" can be a reassuring promise if we are willing to sow only good seeds. It can be a frustrating principle, however, if we insist upon planting weeds and expecting to gather grain.

That's why prayers are so often unanswered. A toddler saw his dad's sharp, shiny straight razor and wanted it. He asked and begged and screamed and stomped. You'd have thought that father was the cruelest man in the world to withhold something so desirable from such a sincere seeker.

Do you think those earnest pleas changed that father's mind? Of course not! He was mature enough to see beyond the bright trinket to the danger and the permanent damage that could result. In this case the child's long-term welfare and his immediate desires were in fatal conflict. His request was denied, not because the father hated him, but because he loved him.

So it is with prayer. Neither God nor nature will aid and abet us in self-destruction. When we say, "Thy will be done," we are saying, "If ultimate good is in conflict with this request, let good prevail even though in my ignorance I may be temporarily disappointed." Only those prayers that represent an authentic desire to line up with God's kingdom purposes are valid.

Now, in the case of this little girl's senseless death, we know God didn't cause it. We also know he didn't nonchalantly allow it. It was not his will that she die, but it was his will that we mature into autonomy. If the human species can expect an occasional abnormal intervention, it will ultimately self-destruct. It is God's love for us that prevents his interference.

Let's think a little deeper into this subject: If God set up a world in which any human carelessness or professional incompetence could be countermanded by divine fiat, we'd never develop responsibility and excellence. God must let us suffer the consequences of our apathy and ineptness or else we'd never change. If God could be summoned in an emergency like a convenient genie, Christians would shrug and say, "Oh well. If worse comes to worse, I can always get God to bail me out!"

Unfortunately, it takes a powerful goad to prod human beings into action. If an evil, sinful, destructive pattern could be reversed by a simple plea to God, then why would anyone exercise care? Why would anyone maintain vigilance? Why would anyone increase their medical skills? Why would anyone devote years of their lives to discover new remedies?

Obviously, no one would! We are lazy creatures, both physically and mentally. The stakes have to be tremendously high to motivate purposeful movement and logical thought. Just how diligent would we be? Just how committed would we be? Just how hard would we really try if we knew God were waiting nearby ready to rush in and miraculously fix things?

God's love has to be tough! He lets us hurt because that's the only way we will learn and grow! If God overrode natural principles and prevented painful consequences, he'd destroy us.

This may help explain why God couldn't take the "cup of death" away from Jesus. He had prayed, "If you are willing" (Luke 22:42). But certain processes had already been set into motion. Particular situations lead to inevitable consequences.

Life is like that. Even though one or many will suffer in a given situation, both nature and God have to be ultimately concerned with the whole. It's significant that the high priest expressed this same insight at the crucifixion. He said, "It is better for you to have one man die for the people than to have the whole nation destroyed" (John 11:50).

This concept is applied in war when soldiers are sacrificed to save a country. It is applied in hostage and kidnapping situations when victims are sacrificed to avoid setting a deadly precedent by providing ransom. It is applied in martyrdoms when the unjust death of one innocent hero rallies people and enables a noble cause to triumph.

Such tough love is also practiced on occasion when caring parents have to let their children learn in the "school of hard knocks," Unfortunately, some things can't be taught; they have to be experienced. Individuals have to try it for themselves. The father let the prodigal son go. He knew failure and pain were inevitable, but that was the only way the son would learn a vital lesson.

Now, how do these principles affect prayer? When voicing concerns to God, when making personal requests, or when facing hard situations that have not been alleviated by prayer, be intelligent and thoughtful rather than submissive or bitter.

Consider God's immutable character.

God is truth. Does reality make the answer you desire impossible?

God is righteous. Do justice and fairness make the answer you desire impossible?

God is love. Does consideration for your own future development and the welfare of others make the answer you desire impossible?

If these crucial principles conflict with your personal interests, adjust your expectations. If a "perfect" solution is unfeasible, consider alternatives. What would be second best? What long-term benefits can be realized from facing the problem? What can you do to bring good from this evil?

God has never solved people's problems for them. God has never promised to do that! He did promise to give believers an enabler so they can solve their own problems. Jesus said, "How much more will the heavenly Father give the Holy Spirit to those who ask him!" (Luke 11:13).

Part 2

God's Natural Principles Constrain His Actions

Before we can determine what hinders prayer, we must analyze the concept of prayer in light of God's natural principles.

Prayer is not a power play or a prescribed ceremony. There are no magic words or proper positions. There are no favored places or special times. Jesus said, "God is spirit, and those who worship him must worship in spirit and truth" (John 4:24).

Prayer, therefore, is an attitude. It involves ultimate concerns and a profound reverence for life. One Hebrew term for prayer suggests self-examination. At its best it is a personal struggle for integrity of character. It's Jacob wrestling with the angel. It's Jeremiah protesting life's injustices. It's the psalmist agonizing in the depth of personal despair.

Jesus said, "Whenever you pray, go into your room and shut the door" (Matt 6:6). We are to face our inadequacies, root out our self-deceits, focus our minds, and verbalize our thoughts. These are enormously important disciplines. Confessing or talking out frustrations leads to inner healing. Prayer lifts our eyes above ourselves and broadens our vision to include others. Prayer is the channel to higher thoughts and better actions. Prayer encourages us to formulate ideals and to imagine more than we can see. When we do this, the contrast between what is and what could be causes such discomfort that we are impelled to move forward.

This compulsion can be very strong, and therein lie some dangers! Christians should always be careful about claiming specific dramatic answers to prayers because it is so easy to make it happen if our spiritual ego is at stake. We ask, and if God doesn't respond, what does that say about us? It says we've failed. It says we're unimportant, unworthy, or ineffective.

These are unpleasant accusations. On the contrary, we all want to prove that we do have an "in" with the boss. We like to demonstrate our leverage in high places. These all too human desires cause us to manufacture events and twist facts to show that God did indeed answer. Some people fall back on the absurd claim that he said, "No!" or "Maybe!" These claims are unfeasible.

Let's examine them in light of the human relationship upon which Jesus based his model of God. Suppose a trusting child approaches his father in a moment of heartbreak. He pours out his soul in anguish. He hurts! His world has collapsed! Yet suppose this father sits in stony silence. No response! No sympathy! No advice! No reassurance! The child would be devastated, and rightly so!

Relationships are based upon empathy and interest. It's obvious that silence isn't a satisfactory response to a hurting soul in either the human realm or the divine realm. People need better explanations. Invalid theology can lead to psychological perversions and social immorality.

A magazine reported the story of a boy whose face was eaten away by a rare disease: "Horribly disfigured, little David faced a cruel and lonely death in the jungles of Peru—locked in a cage by natives who believed his hideously deformed face was a punishment from God. Only a few who pitied him and pushed scraps of food through the bars of his cage kept him alive. Just one word described his pitiful fate: Doomed."

Fortunately, a Scottish physician saw him and is restoring his features, but the horrifying part is that as long as the people believed God had afflicted him, they felt no compassion or responsibility.

Many primitive people actually believed God imposed such mindless punishment. Many modern people stop short of these awful claims, but they are still confused. A recent headline read: "Mother Left with Pain and Bitterness." Her only daughter had been brutally murdered. She said, "I was awake and waiting for my daughter to come home by a 12:30 a.m. curfew. She never arrived. The real hurt is missing her. And it's horrible how she died…stabbed. How could anybody treat another human being like that? I've lost my faith in God completely. He didn't take her; the devil did. But he should have kept me from going through this."

The mother doesn't say, "God did it," but she thinks he "allowed" it. There is really no difference! If he can prevent suffering and doesn't, he is still accountable: "Anyone, then, who knows the right thing to do and fails to do it commits sin" (Jas 4:17). Therefore, if God can cure cancer, why doesn't he? If God can deflect tornadoes from churches and hospitals, why doesn't he? If God can keep car accidents from mangling children's bodies, why doesn't he?

These impossible theological and ethical impasses create a threatening and debilitating problem. Psychologists say that since human beings can't live with dissonance, we must either assimilate or accommodate. That means we must fix one thing or the other. We either adjust reality to fit our preconceptions or we adjust our preconceptions to fit reality. In short, if no solutions can be found, then honest, perceptive individuals are forced to either nullify and pervert their rational system or nullify and pervert their moral system.

Since both systems are vital to life, we can't sacrifice either one and survive, so most of us limp along trying to ignore the incongruities. We rationalize away the conflicts, suppress the anxieties, and deny the resentments that result.

Under these conditions we are unable to fully utilize either our rational or our moral system, and this makes us less than healthy, productive persons.

Again, it's paradoxical that the very principles of the universe upon which we depend—unity, consistency, and progression—actually constrain God's actions.

Unity

A busload of excited young people and adults left the small rural church. They were off for the trip of their lifetime. Many in the group had saved and sacrificed to afford even the nominal expense of the tour. A world's fair was being held about a thousand miles away, and some of these travelers had never had an opportunity to attend even a state fair, much less an international one. A great deal of planning and penny-pinching had gone into this endeavor. The congregation was trying to allow as many members as possible to participate.

The trip went well, and anticipation mounted. The children looked forward to the rides and science exhibits. Some wanted to shop in the foreign bazaar; others simply hoped to photograph their unique experiences. The group stayed overnight in a small town nearby to save on motel expenses. They drove in early in order to get the maximum benefit from their all-day tickets. Finally, the bus was parked, and the passengers climbed out to begin their adventure.

Just as they approached the entrance gate, the rains came. Black clouds seemed to empty themselves on the tourists. Once inside, the drenched travelers huddled under the trees and canopies, fully expecting the shower to pass. It never did. Their one day was totally ruined. Their one educational and cultural opportunity was completely lost. Displays closed early. Photography was impossible. The toddlers sneezed, and the senior citizens ached. Why couldn't God have delayed or moved this rainstorm? The entire church as well as the group involved had prayed for the success of this trip. There were elderly ladies along who would never be able to attend another fair. This wasn't a "blessing in disguise." This wasn't an "advantageous experience." It was simply a waste! Why couldn't God have modified the weather?

To understand the answer to this question, we must consider the fact that God's natural principles constrain his actions. This world is interconnected. You can't change or fix one little isolated piece without ruining the whole. If a single piece of a puzzle is mutilated, nothing fits! If a single block of a Rubik's Cube is out of place, nothing is right! If a single figure is wrong in an accountant's books, nothing will balance! A single sore toe can throw your whole body out of line! God's creation must exhibit unity. The scripture says, "There is one God, the Father, from whom are all things and for whom we exist, and one Lord, Jesus Christ, through whom are all things and through whom we exist" (1 Cor 8:6).

All of God's natural laws must be mutually supportive. Jesus emphasized this vital concept, saying, "If a kingdom is divided against itself, that kingdom cannot stand. And if a house is divided against itself, that house will not be able to stand" (Mark 3:24–25).

A unified universe is important. It allows us to draw parallels between the physical and the spiritual worlds. It verifies the validity of parables. It enables us to construct tangible models to analyze intangible ideas. Scientific experiments and technological analysis depend upon a unified universe. If everything fits, if life is "of a piece," then we can freely transfer knowledge between various areas.

God's creative force is systematic and harmonious. Paul said, "In him all things in heaven and on earth were created, things visible and invisible, whether thrones or dominions or rulers or powers—all things have been created through him and for him. He himself is before all things, and in him all things hold together" (Col 1:16–17).

The ethical development of the Greeks and Romans was hindered because they believed the gods in heaven and the human beings on earth operated from totally different perspectives. The pagan deities admonished human beings to "do as we say do, not as we do." The Israelites, on the other hand, made tremendous theological and moral progress because they rightly understood that God operates in heaven and on earth the same. The scripture says, "So acknowledge today and take to heart that the LORD is God in heaven above and on the earth beneath; there is no other" (Deut 4:39). Jesus said, "Be perfect, therefore, as your heavenly Father is perfect" (Matt 5:48).

Few things of value are ever created by committees or institutions. Instead, most discoveries and accomplishments are made by individuals with focus and discipline. A project that has one strong person behind it will be stable, uniform, and balanced. It will have integrity, coherence, and symmetry.

This universe is a marvelous example of order and harmony because one mind conceived it and one will created it. The scripture says, "Thus says the LORD, who created the heavens (he is God!), who formed the earth and made it (he established it; he did not create it a chaos; he formed it to be inhabited!): 'I am the LORD, and there is no other'" (Isa 45:18).

This oneness, or unity, permeates and influences all of life. Paul said, "There is one body and one Spirit, just as you were called to the one hope of your calling, one Lord, one faith, one baptism, one God and Father of all, who is above all and through all and in all" (Eph 4:4–6).

Most people do not think these kinds of thoughts because they seem academic and impractical. They are not! Instead, they are very real and very practical. They affect all we do.

Now, what relevance does a unified universe have in the matter of prayer? It is relevant because many of our prayers are childish, selfish, and personally oriented. Jesus said, "You do not know what you are asking" (Matt 20:22). How true that is! We'd bring chaos to the universe if all our prayers were answered!

Sincere people often pray vehemently on different sides of a war, on different sides of a political campaign, and on different sides of a social issue. An old rabbi tells the story of a woman who has two sons. One, a gardener, begs, "O, Mother, pray for rain to water my plants." The other, a potter, begs, "O, Mother, pray for sunshine to dry my pots." The mother loves them equally. Should she pray for rain or sunshine?

This simple tale identifies a complex problem. Petitions that would require fragmentation of the universe can never be answered. One law cannot nullify another. One principle cannot repudiate another. Petitions that would pit one section of creation against another can never be answered. Petitions that would set heaven in competition with earth can never be answered.

Not only is the cosmos or physical creation unified; mankind also shares a common relatedness. As fellow human beings we are all interconnected. No man can keep the consequences of his life, either good or evil, strictly to himself. What we are and what we do affects our families, our communities, our nation, and our world. If a person could sin privately, then he might allow himself some perverted self-indulgence, but he cannot. Somebody else is always involved. Indeed, the whole universe is involved. A wicked person has deprived the world of a good life and given it a bad life instead. Sinning contaminates the public reservoir. Sooner or later, everybody suffers from the pollution.

In Shakespeare's play *Richard III*, the Duke of Clarence says, "O God, if my deep prayers cannot appease Thee, Thou wilt be avenged on my misdeeds, yet execute Thy wrath on me alone!" This sounds magnanimous, but it is a futile request. God cannot grant it. No person ever bears all the consequences of his own sin!

Fortunately, the same laws of unity also operate in a more positive vein. The fact that life is an entity gives credence to the suffering servant symbol. It explains to some extent how a single man can die for an entire group of people, and it sheds some light on the principles involved in intercessory prayer.

Since we believe our God is one, in whom all live and move and have their being, we realize that the power of prayer may activate personal influence even at a distance. To say this effect is psychological is only another way of saying God has so arranged mental and social laws that a concentrated expression of concern by earnest people brings results. We may discover that empathy and even mental telepathy play a role. In any case, the whole idea of intercession is dependent upon the stability of natural laws. If all things are unified, you can't change any one thing without changing other things, and therein lies the value of intercessory prayer.

Getting one piece of a jigsaw puzzle in its proper place makes it easier to fit the others. Likewise, if even one individual will align himself properly with kingdom purposes, he makes it easier for others to do the same. "No man is an island," they say. Indeed, no object is an island. No idea is an island. Everything is meshed. Everything eventually affects everything else.

Scientists give us some startling facts about the physical universe. The moon affects the ocean tides. The gravitational pull of the stars and planets affects the orbits of other bodies light years away. The influence of one thing upon another is almost unbelievable.

Jesus said the same thing is true in the spiritual world. A tiny sparrow's falling is noted in the divine annals (see Matt 10:29). Negative thoughts, idle words, and small deeds are influential. If one word is wrong in a crossword puzzle, it can't be solved. If a rocket is off course a hair's breadth at the launch pad, it will be off course a million miles by the time it gets to the infinity of space.

Negative thoughts affect our own character, and inevitably this negativity spreads to others. The scripture says, "On that day thoughts will come into your mind, and you will devise an evil scheme. You will say, 'I will go up against the land of unwalled villages; I will fall upon the quiet people who live in safety, all of them living without walls and having no bars or gates, to seize spoil and to carry off plunder'" (Ezek 38:10–12).

Evil thoughts lead to evil words, and words can't be unsaid. Once soundwaves have been set into motion, they can't be recalled. We can clarify, retract, or apologize, but the damage has already been done. The destruction can be mitigated, but it can't be abolished.

This illustrates the fact that seemingly insignificant statements have eternal significance. Jesus knew this when he said, "On the day of judgment you will have to give an account for every careless word you utter" (Matt 12:36).

We cannot undo our bad deeds or take back our unkind actions. When a pebble is dropped into the water, the ripple effect spreads inexorably toward the banks of the stream. It never reverses itself. It's only in movies that events and processes can be run backwards to return to the point of origin as if they had never occurred.

Even small deeds are important because they aid in kingdom purposes. Jesus said, "Whoever gives even a cup of cold water to one of these little ones in the name of a disciple—truly I tell you, none of these will lose their reward" (Matt 10:42). Things are infinitely more complex than we realize. Even the individual hairs on our head have numerical significance (see Matt 10:30).

In God's response to Job, God tried to raise Job's eyes to the bigger picture, encouraging him to see the natural rather than the personal: "The LORD answered Job out of the whirlwind: 'Where were you when I laid the foundation of the earth?... Have you comprehended the expanse of the earth? Declare, if you know all this.... Do you know the ordinances of the heavens? Can you establish their rule on the earth?" (Job 38:1, 4, 18, 33).

When Job began to realize the majesty and unity of the universe, he was satisfied. The same thing can happen to us. When we become mature enough and enlightened enough to see the whole, then we'll understand why certain personal prayers can't be answered. God's processes depend on continuity and interrelatedness. If he tampered with the weather at one spot for our particular individual benefit, he'd destroy the overall balance and harmony of nature. God's permanent unity is more important than our temporary desires.

Consistency

On a dark, rainy night in early spring, a church music director was leading a revival in a nearby city. His wife and son stayed home because the child had a cold. While driving to the services, the minister was involved in a horrible automobile accident. An oncoming car lost control, crossed the center line, and hit him head on. The handsome, dedicated, talented young man was pronounced dead on arrival at his hometown hospital. The careless motorist, a middle-aged businessman, received only minor injuries.

What a tragedy and what a dilemma for conscientious Christians. Where was God? Even as well-meaning church members murmured piously, "The Lord giveth, and the Lord taketh away; he knows best," they didn't mean it! The family couldn't believe that! God ordained that parents are to be honored and blessed by their children, yet an aged father and mother are left without their only son. God ordained marriage because it is not good for one to live alone, yet this young wife is a widow. God ordained families because children need the strong influence of adult guidance, yet this little boy will have no father during his formative years. God ordained religious leaders, yet this church is left with no one to fill a crucial role in the areas of youth and music. There are so few with these abilities.

This situation is not for the best. Everyone knows it! We're lying to ourselves when we claim that it is! Are we saying that God wanted this to happen? Did he set up this experience? Did he cause the church to hold a revival and ask this particular person to lead it? Did he make the businessman turn the wheel into the opposite lane? Did he reduce the unfortunate young man's reflexes? Did he strengthen the steel of the other car so that driver wouldn't be killed? Of course not!

Yet these are the very things we insinuate when we make sanctimonious statements concerning fate and God's sovereignty. Most people today will say, "Oh, God didn't actually do the destructive deed; he merely removed his protective hand." Do you mean he blinked at the wrong moment? Did he decide this just wasn't to be the victim's lucky day? In other words, were some believers on some highways that night afforded special divine protection while this one was not? If this is so, then the next question must be, "Why wasn't he blessed? Why was he left out? Did he forget to pray prior to his trip? Did he neglect to hang a cross in his car? Did his friends leave him out of their intercessory petitions? Did the family fail to invoke God's guidance that evening?"

If any of these statements are true, then how many prayers would it have taken to contact God and activate his supernatural forces? If anyone at all is spared by divine intervention, then God is like a switchboard operator sitting before a control panel in a burning hotel. He could push a button and turn on the sprinkler system in any room, but instead of quickly and compassionately saving everyone, he says, "Now let me see. I believe I'll save numbers 110 and 230 tonight and let the others burn to death." This is an utterly abominable response. God doesn't do that!

To understand any of the apparent incongruities, we must examine God's natural principles. These constrain his actions. God's creation must exhibit consistency. The scripture says, "I the LORD do not change" (Mal 3:6).

Consistency suggests efficiency and consonance, an organization of all parts. The separate aspects agree with each other. They fit like pieces of a jigsaw puzzle. They mesh like cogs in a well-oiled machine. There is no friction to impede the operation. There is no dissension among the various factions. We can rely on certain facts. Processes that work in the natural realm will work in the spiritual realm. Methods that are effective in social practices will be effective in spiritual practice. There is a cosmic commonality. Scientists say, "The same elements of matter and laws of physics are found throughout the known universe."

How does an understanding of the consistency of God's natural principles affect our prayers? We are able to pray more intelligently when we realize the one axiom that God is immutable. The scripture says, "With [God] there is no variation or shadow due to change" (Jas 1:17). Another verse reads, "Jesus Christ is the same yesterday and today and forever" (Heb 13:8).

Prayer doesn't change God; it changes us! When sailors in a small boat throw an anchor onto a rock, they may seem to be pulling the rock toward them, but actually they are pulling themselves toward the rock. So it is in prayer. We are not pulling God over to our viewpoint. We are pulling ourselves toward his!

Do we really expect to change God's mind or influence his actions? Do we really expect to get his pity or talk him into something?

Too often, prayer has been used as a superstition, a charm, a rabbit's foot. We don't want to take any chances, so we whisper a prayer as we cross our fingers. Prayer is used as a means of last resort—"When all else fails, pray!" We wave a religious wand, press a sacred button, rub a holy lamp, ring for a divine bellhop, summon a heavenly genie to do our bidding. Prayer is for emergencies. When we goof up, we expect God to bail us out.

These concepts are invalid. Prayer doesn't change things; it changes us so we can change things!

The very fact that our spirit can commune with God affirms our worth and enables us to achieve wonderful victories, but are these accomplishments supernatural? That depends upon our use of the phrase. Words mean different things to different people, and a definition of terms is essential. If by *supernatural* we mean "going against the natural world," if we mean "contradicting reality," if we mean "breaking or twisting the orderly principles of life," then it is not of God. Such processes would be whimsical and destructive. Jesus said a house divided can't stand (see Matt 12:25). God can't make rules and then nullify them. Once he decided on certain gravitational and chemical reactions, these can't be changed. Science, technology, and life itself depend upon a trustworthy universe.

On the other hand, if by *supernatural* we mean "raising the natural world to its highest potential," if we mean "discovering and understanding every aspect of reality," if we mean "utilizing the orderly principles of life to their fullest," then the supernatural is not only possible but imperative for progress.

Supernatural doesn't mean going against nature; it means going beyond nature. Therefore, every accomplishment of man is supernatural. It is natural for weeds to grow in gardens. It is natural for plagues to wipe out nations. It is natural for a high percentage of babies to die in infancy. In all areas of life, mankind has gone beyond the natural!

Prayer involves the problem of natural law versus events labeled as miracles. How can God shape the course of nature and human history without interfering with his laws? Is it possible that what we call a miracle need not break, cancel, or supersede ordinary principles? Let's consider agriculture. If you plant a rock and a seed side by side, it is the nature of the pebble to remain inanimate while it is the nature of the seed to grow. If, therefore, the rock could see the seed sprouting, it might shout in astonishment, "Behold, a miracle!" Of course we know that no law has been overridden. There, as in most cases, what some call a miracle is simply the fulfilling of a larger or higher law that they don't yet understand. For instance, to natives from tropical regions, water becoming solid overnight would be a miracle. We call it freezing and understand the reason behind the phenomenon. To eighteenth-century people, the idea of men floating around in space would be a miracle. We call it weightlessness and understand the reasons behind the phenomenon.

Radios, televisions, cellphones, and the internet would definitely have been miraculous to people in the first or even the nineteenth century. Natural law is the human explanation of how things regularly happen. In a world where every cause has an effect and every effect has a cause, it is absurd to expect God to change things just to suit us. In a world where each action is intertwined with all other actions and inevitable consequences result from previous actions, it is absurd to ask God to stop the world on our behalf!

In this area there is much confusion. The Bible assumes the existence of God and the naturalness of prayer, but men in a pre-scientific age could not answer, or even ask, the questions that confront men in a scientific-technological age. Primitive people saw no difficulty in a fleece on the same night becoming both wet and dry (see Judg 3:37ff.). They believed the sun could stop and then proceed (see Josh 10:13). They didn't consider the effect this would have on people around the world. In fact, they didn't even know there were people on the other side of the world. They thought the shadow on the sundial could go forward or backward (see Isa 38:8). They imagined an ax head could choose to either sink or float (see 2 Kgs 6:5ff.).

Like all people of the generations during which the Bible was being written, the prophets and disciples observed and described events in terms of miracle and not of law. They had no understanding of causes and effects.

This increases the perplexity of many modern Christians. That world is not ours. There is no place on this earth today where we cannot depend on nature's regularity. We predict sunrise and sunset to the second, and they never fail. We chart the course of the planets and stars, and they are never late. The achievements of our modern age rest on the assurance that we can always rely on the same things happening under the same conditions.

Natural law, however, is not as absolutely determined as superficial thinking makes it appear to be. Understanding both scientific and spiritual principles is like going through a long tunnel. If you go in only a short distance, there's darkness and restriction. Those who become fearful and stop at that point will remain limited and frustrated. Those who are brave enough to go a little farther, however, will find light and liberty. An open road with unbelievable possibilities lies ahead!

People with a little knowledge of physics would say, "Water can't run uphill. It's against natural law." That's not quite true, because as a matter of fact, we see water run uphill every day! Huge tanks are built on mountaintops; high pumping stations are established. The water runs up and down with equal facility and easily reaches the upper stories of the tallest buildings.

This illustrates an important principle. It's true that people can't violate the law of gravitation, but they can use the law of gravitation! By combining our intelligence and ingenuity with nature's consistent laws, we can accomplish great things. Likewise, a heavy substance can't float upon a light one, yet every day steel ships cross the ocean and metal airplanes fill the skies.

Again, it is true that people can never break or change laws, but they can utilize these forces to do what the natural elements could never do by themselves. When an engineer proposes to bridge a river, an unenlightened person might say, "That's impossible. The natural laws forbid you from hanging iron over air!" The engineer, with deeper insight, could reply, "Yes, but natural laws can be used as well as obeyed. The very inviolability of the laws makes them useful. They are dependable. They can be trusted. They are the same yesterday, today, and forever."

Even though these laws are unchanging, we as intelligent human beings are not. People can manipulate and utilize the energies of nature until millions of travelers can cross rivers on their bridges.

When people consider the inflexibility of laws, they are thinking of causes and effects as forming a rigid system, but in practical experience we deal with different kinds of causes. When the atmospheric pressure makes the wind blow, that is one kind. When a man sails by that same wind, skillfully using it to reach his destination, that is another kind. In one case we have an absolutely predetermined procedure; in the other we have a personal will utilizing the predetermined procedure to serve our purposes.

These two kinds of causes are at work everywhere. When snow falls on the sidewalk, its removal may be affected by natural causes, such as sunshine or rain. Its removal may also be affected by "supernatural" causes, such as a man with a shovel or a snowplow. Natural laws are consistent. If the temperature rises, the snow melts. Prayer won't change that fact. We can refrigerate it so it won't melt, but that doesn't break the law concerning thirty-two degrees Fahrenheit. If the temperature doesn't rise, the snow won't melt. Prayers won't change that fact. We can heat it so it will melt; again, that doesn't break the law concerning thirty-two degrees Fahrenheit.

In short, man, utilizing divine wisdom, adds the super to the natural. All human achievements are illustrations of this truth. That's how prayers are answered.

The talented young music director was killed because natural laws were broken. If God had intervened between causes and effects, the consistency of the universe would be undermined.

Progression

A young naval officer and his wife were expecting their first child. Both loved children, and everyone was especially delighted since there were no other babies in either one's immediate family. All went well. An ordinary and uneventful pregnancy ended on time with a fast trip to the hospital. The prospective grandmother accompanied the mother-to-be since her husband was stationed on the East Coast.

A normal birth occurred, but then the trouble began. There was a long delay and several strange consultations. The anxious relatives were not allowed to see the baby. The absent father was contacted by the Red Cross. When he arrived after a harried night flight, a meeting was called. The young parents were informed that their beautiful little girl had a rare genetic defect. She could not live! To make the situation worse, the couple was told that their chances of ever having a normal baby were slight.

Here is the situation. A dedicated Christian man and woman—desperately wanting to give love, nurture, and education to a child—can't have one, while millions of other uncaring men and women are having abortions, abandoning newborns, and abusing toddlers.

They prayed! Their families prayed! Their chaplain prayed! Their church members prayed! But the baby died! Why didn't God answer?

Before we can understand any of life's awful moments, we have to examine God's natural principles God's creation must exhibit progression. Many scriptures describe this expectation. Peter said, "In accordance with his promise, we wait for new heavens and a new earth, where righteousness is at home" (2 Pet 3:13).

There is an ultimate goal ahead. Life moves in only one direction. It cannot go backward. Evil is never rewarded and therefore must eventually become extinct. Good is always rewarded and therefore must eventually become predominant. The pointer for this system originates in Genesis. The scripture says, "God saw everything that he had made, and indeed, it was very good" (Gen 1:31).

Not only was God's creative work good in the beginning; his goodness continues. The psalmist said, "He loves righteousness and justice; the earth is full of the steadfast love of the LORD" (Ps 33:5).

To progress means to advance, to develop, to grow, to move forward, to increase, and to improve. These are all desirable objectives. Those people who allow God's progressive principles to work in their lives can participate in this maturing process. Paul said, "I am confident of this, that the one who began a good work in you will continue to complete it" (Phil 1:6).

Even more importantly, events, circumstances, and failures can be shaped toward positive accomplishment. Paul said, "We know that all things work together for good for those who love God, who are called according to his purpose" (Rom 8:28).

What does the progressive nature of God's natural principles have to do with our prayers? The key to this dilemma lies in the conditional statement of Jesus: "I will do whatever you ask in my name" (John 14:13). Now, contrary to many people's belief, *in Jesus's name* isn't a secret code phrase to be tacked onto our shopping list of requests. *In my name* means, in my nature, compatible with my character, according to God's overall plan.

It's significant that even Jesus didn't try to use God for personal benefit. He wouldn't turn stones into bread or invoke divine protection in foolhardy endeavors, like leaping from the pinnacle of the temple (see Matt 4:1–7). Therefore, those who pray in Jesus's name must always take into account natural laws, scientific principles, and a sense of reality. To pray in Jesus's name, we must be honest. Honest Christians don't bend truth and twist facts. Honest Christians don't try to make God a partner in "get rich quick" schemes.

To pray in Jesus's name, we must be mature. Mature Christians know there are no shortcuts in life. Mature Christians know God won't override the principles of natural law and human effort.

Jesus said, "My Father is still working, and I also am working" (John 5:17). Likewise, we must join God in labor instead of asking him to join us in magical endeavors or indolence.

Obviously, prayers that diminish life cannot be honored because God won't aid and abet us in processes that would sabotage his kingdom or hinder its progression! Some personal petitions pervert the ultimate purpose of prayer. Children say, "I want that now!" and "What did you get me?" When they become mature adults, their desires broaden and deepen.

Too often, if we did receive answers to our short-sighted, selfish prayers, they would cause more harm than good. Many requests would be counterproductive. King Midas thought he wanted everything he touched to turn to gold, but when his wish was granted, he was devastated to see his food and his flowers become rigid. He was horrified to see his pets and finally his only daughter turned from warm flesh into cold metal.

People complain of unanswered prayers, but there would be far greater disasters if all of mankind's foolish prayers were answered. Quite often, we get into trouble as a result of getting what we thought we wanted. When the prodigal, in the far country, came to himself, his friends were gone, his reputation was gone, his money was gone, and his health was gone. He was suffering from the effects of having a dominant wish fulfilled.

Lot looked toward the city and wanted Sodom. He got it and was almost destroyed in the process. Ahab craved Naboth's vineyard. He got it and lost everything in the process. Judas wanted thirty pieces of silver. He got them and traded away his soul in the process.

It's obvious that the purpose of prayer is not just to obtain our heart's desires, but rather to examine the inner motives that prompt these desires. The purpose of prayer is not just to change circumstances, but rather to enable us to use and overcome circumstances.

We must not expect God to bail us out. The Greek dramatists often developed plots so complicated that the characters become hopelessly entangled, incapable of solving their dilemmas by human ingenuity. When this happened, the stagehands would use a mechanical device to swing in a god to untangle the desperate situation.

In reality, God won't run interference or turn back the clock.

Now, what does God's natural principles concerning progression have to do with answers to prayers? It has everything to do with them. The young couple's baby died because understanding and applying progressive and constructive principles are up to us. The power to answer that particular prayer does not lie with God. It lies with those determined scientists who are only now beginning to discover genetic links. It lies with those gifted thinkers who are gradually developing fertility techniques. It lies with those dedicated doctors who are preventing or mitigating prenatal problems.

If God gave one unearned insight or magically fixed one biological defect, we'd never search and struggle again! The person expecting to be fed won't work nearly so hard as the person who knows beyond a doubt that he will starve if he doesn't get food through his own efforts. The entire universe is set up on the premise that it is through humanity's energetic input that life will become progressively more productive. Any interference will either retard growth or reverse the positive movement. God expressly delegated this role to man in the very beginning. The scripture says, "God blessed them, and God said to them, 'Be fruitful and multiply and fill the earth and subdue it and have dominion over the fish of the sea and over the birds of the air and over every living thing that moves upon the earth'" (Gen 1:28).

This means we are to take charge and assume control. Mitigating earthly ills is not God's job; it's our job! Utilizing earthly products is not God's job; it's our job! We're to heal the sick, feed the hungry, clothe the poor (see Matt 10:8).

Three old proverbial sayings illustrate this theology: "Pray devoutly, but hammer stoutly"; "Don't pray for lighter burdens but for stronger backs"; "God helps those who help themselves."

Dwight L. Moody was on a boat that was taking in water and sinking. Sailors, knowing he was a preacher, said, "Quick! Kneel and pray!" Moody retorted, "I can pray while I pass the buckets."

The old adage is true: "Pray as if it all depends upon God, and work as if it all depends upon you." The adage is true because most things do depend on both God and man. God provides the ores, but man must mine and refine them. God provides the seeds, but man must plant and harvest them. God provides the resources, but man must discover and develop them.

During the dry season in the New Hebrides, a missionary was ridiculed by the natives when he started digging for water. They said, "Everybody knows water always comes down from heaven. Water never comes up from the earth." The missionary, however, who had more knowledge and information, revealed a larger truth. He persisted and finally demonstrated clearly that water could indeed be obtained through different channels.

Many religious people are just as shortsighted as these natives. They insist upon waiting for God to send answers, solutions, and blessings in a supernatural way when all the time an abundant supply is available from natural sources if they can simply learn to recognize them and exert their own efforts to take advantage of them.

The familiar story of the drowning man illustrates this principle: A flood washed a town away, and one pious deacon was forced to take refuge on his roof. A rowboat came by and offered assistance. "No!" the victim replied. "I'm trusting in God. He'll save me."

The water rose higher! A motorboat came by and offered assistance. "No!" the victim replied. "I'm trusting in God. He'll save me!"

The water came to his chin, and a helicopter flew over and offered assistance. "No!" the victim replied again. "I'm trusting in God. He'll save me!"

Finally, he drowned. When he reached heaven, he was furious. Shaking his finger in God's face, he complained, "I trusted you, and you let me drown."

God answered, "Why, man, what did you expect? I sent you two boats and a helicopter!"

Too often, we don't see God in the ordinary, but Jesus did! To him, God was in lilies, children, and loving concern, not in farfetched signs.

Too many people feel they have to manufacture miracles to prove God. We see a black cow eat green grass and give white milk. Zoologists identify hundreds of coordinated muscles in a tiny caterpillar's head. Our own brain processes and stores innumerable memories per second, and we still need "supernatural" miracles? Surely we can find enough support for genuine reverence in the unity, consistency, and progression of God's natural principles, rather than in aberrations and interventions.

Which engineer would you respect more, the one who can build a factory that works flawlessly century after century or the one who builds a factory that has to have periodic electric shocks to jar it into operation?

Emphasizing human efforts and accomplishments doesn't minimize the importance of God and faith! If you have no confidence in God's providence and no belief in possibilities, you have no hope; without hope, all is lost. Hope is closely akin to faith. Faith motivates the determined effort, and the determined effort is what achieves the goal. Pearl divers must have faith that there are such things as pearls and that they have the possibility of finding them or they'd never search. Gold miners must have faith that there are such things as gold nuggets and that they have the possibility of finding them or they'd never dig. Research scientists must have faith that there are solutions to life's problems and that they have the possibility of finding them or they'd never experiment.

Those who see the ravages of cancer and shake their heads, saying, "I just don't think we were meant to know!" will never discover a cure. A stubborn faith pulls us like a magnet and pushes us like a bulldozer. It won't let us quit! In other words, if we don't believe something can be done, we won't try. Furthermore, if we don't believe we have a fair chance of doing it, we won't try. Faith is essential!

Part 3

God's Gift of Human Freedom Constrains His Action

Before we can determine what hinders prayer, we must analyze the concept of prayer in light of God's gift of human freedom.

Prayer is a broad term covering the whole area of interchange between the physical and the spiritual worlds. It includes personal growth and constructive action. Prayers, as traditionally understood, seldom effect dramatic, immediate, overt results because life is interwoven and complex. In answering prayers God must work through imperfect earthly channels and utilize immature human capacities. Otherwise, he undermines our development. As one character said in the play *Green Pastures*, "That's the trouble with passing a miracle. Once you start, there's no place to stop!"

Prayer isn't a magic button, but it does pave the way. It voices our desires. It focuses our attention. It directs our minds. Most importantly, it gives God permission to enter our lives. We may not realize it, but because we are free, autonomous agents, God does nothing by coercion! He doesn't intrude or force his resources upon us. His hands are tied until we request his assistance.

When we pray, we are saying, in effect, "It's okay, God. I'm inviting you into this situation. I'm asking for your help. If anything can be done through me, I'm open. I'm receptive. I'm willing to move as the Holy Spirit guides." Such a prayer allows God's wisdom to penetrate our minds. The illumination is often gradual because we are slow to understand and many extraneous factors are involved.

Finding the "mind of God" is not as simple as closing your eyes and pointing to a verse of scripture. Nevertheless, prayer is still our best method of bringing divine powers into play.

Realizing our part in the process helps explain the puzzling statement Jesus made concerning prayer: "When you are praying, do not heap up empty phrases as the gentiles do, for they think that they will be heard because of their many words. Do not be like them, for your Father knows what you need before you ask him" (Matt 6:7–8).

When considering such passages, thinking people have always raised this question: "If God knows what we need and wants us to have it, what's stopping him?" In other words, why would a loving Father have to be begged before he will give good gifts? In fact, God doesn't have to be reminded or persuaded, but he does have to find agents through whom to work. If we won't give, go, teach, and share, he can do nothing! It's up to us, or else the great commission is a farce!

This brings up some basic questions: What powers control the events of life on this earth? Is there any rhyme or reason to our existence? Who sets up the inevitable chain of causes and effects? Why are they set up in certain ways? Are God's purposes predetermined?

In searching for answers to these and other profound questions, the Gospel record gives us some clues. When Jesus went back to his hometown, Nazareth, the scriptures say, "He could do no deed of power there" (Mark 6:5). Was the Lord of all living limited? Could the Savior of the world be frustrated and stymied by mere men? Furthermore, if Jesus was exemplifying God, then is God also limited?

Let's think about the blind beggars in the days of Jesus. Were all of them healed? Not by any means! Down in Jericho one day, blind Bartimaeus cried out, "Son of David, help me! Help me!" (see Mark 10:46–52). He was rewarded. Jesus responded to all who called upon him. The record is one hundred percent consistent. On the other hand, he didn't help any of those who didn't call upon him! He never walked up to a suffering sinner and said, "Brother, I'm going to heal you," or "Sister, I'm going to fix you!"

These examples show that specific encounters must originate at our end of the line. God doesn't instigate changes in us. He reaches out through the initiative of his grace, but he doesn't invade! He responds, but he doesn't coerce! It's important for us to do the asking, because in this way our freedom is protected.

There is no indication that God ever bestows things arbitrarily or "out of the blue." He doesn't pick one to enrich and one to impoverish. He doesn't choose one to rescue and one to neglect. The prodigal's father didn't go to the hog pen and rescue his son. It's true that he was waiting with arms outstretched, eager to accept and bless, but the first move had to come from the wanderer himself (see Luke 15:20). Jesus didn't go to Bethany at Lazarus's death until Martha and Mary sent for him (see John 11:3). He didn't help Jairus's daughter until he was specifically invited to enter into their sorrow (see Mark 5:22–24).

In the parable of the neighbor who needed three loaves of bread, we're told he had to describe his situation precisely and persist in the only course that could satisfy his needs before the reward came (see Luke 11:5–8).

In light of these scriptures, we can see that prayer has often been defined too narrowly. We talk about "saying our prayers," but a constant state of acute awareness is also prayer. A constant attitude of receptiveness is prayer. A constant willingness to learn, grow, and change is prayer. A lifestyle that "lets God in" is prayer. Meditation or thinking is prayer. God's voice often speaks through our own conscience and our own highest ideals.

God doesn't control us, but he does extend calls to service. Therefore, listening is prayer. The scripture says, "The LORD came and stood there, calling as before, 'Samuel! Samuel!' And Samuel said, 'Speak, for your servant is listening'" (1 Sam 3:10).

Some little boys were marching, beating drums, and blowing whistles. Suddenly, one of them yelled, "Beat louder! Beat louder! I think I hear my daddy calling me, and I don't want to hear him!"

How often do we do that? An inner urge compels us to positive action, and we repress it, deny it, or ignore it. We get busy, turn up the level of our economic involvement, and bury ourselves in social activities because we don't want to hear!

The still small voice of our conscience must not be stifled. God doesn't yell; he whispers. Elijah didn't find him in whirlwinds and earthquakes but in a still small voice (see 1 Kgs 19:12–13).

It's paradoxical that the very gift of God we appreciate so much—the human freedom to be, to think, and to do—can actually constrain his actions.

Being

They were an outstandingly attractive couple. The man's dark curly hair and trim physique drew attention in any crowd. The woman was also unusually pretty, but she seemed anxious and slightly withdrawn. Three demure little girls were picture perfect outwardly, but underneath they seemed subdued and fearful. Unfortunately, this ideal American family had a serious problem. The young husband was an alcoholic. When he drank, he was violent and abusive.

The woman and children were faithful Christians. They, their church, and indeed the entire community prayed fervently about the situation, but it continued to worsen. The man beat his daughters, threatened his wife, and almost killed his invalid mother.

Finally, one Sunday night during services, he stormed into the church with a loaded rifle. In his wild rage he was bent upon shooting everyone in sight, but especially his family. They ran into the pastor's study and out a side door into the parsonage. Some men overpowered the madman and held him until the police came and hauled him off to jail.

After serving a short sentence he got out, searching everywhere for his wife and girls, still determined to kill them. For many years they were literally prisoners of their fear in a free country, living in hiding, moving frequently, and keeping their whereabouts secret from even close friends.

In the meantime the derelict terrorized his family, embarrassed his relatives, and made obscene phone calls to pastors and church leaders who had known his wife. In short, for twenty years he made life miserable for all concerned. He never contributed or provided anything of value and finally died at the age of fifty.

Now, why weren't all the prayers in his behalf answered? Before we can make an intelligent response, we must analyze God's methods.

His gift of human freedom constrains his actions. God can't make people be something against their will. He said, "I have called and you refused, have stretched out my hand and no one heeded.... They hated knowledge and did not choose the fear of the LORD" (Prov 1:24, 29). God can't superimpose positive qualities and attitudes. Such things have to be internally developed.

We must do the choosing. God said, "I call heaven and earth to witness against you today that I have set before you life and death, blessings and curses. Choose life so that you and your descendants may live" (Deut 30:19).

We must do the seeking: "Seek good and not evil, that you may live" (Amos 5:14).

We must do the coming: "The Spirit and the bride say, 'Come.' And let everyone who hears say, 'Come.' And let everyone who is thirsty come. Let anyone who wishes take the water of life as a gift" (Rev 22:17).

Our relationship to God as children, not robots, is significant. Our position before God as autonomous individuals, not manipulated puppets, is significant. Our status before God as envoys, not slaves, is significant. That's why the determination of the results of our intercessory prayers often resides in those for whom we pray, not in God.

The rich young ruler was allowed to walk away because he possessed God's gift of freedom. Jesus loved him, yearned for him, and earnestly desired his allegiance, but he could not and would not force him to make a commitment. Likewise, the determination of the results of most personal prayers resides in us. Jesus said, "Believe that you have received it, and it will be yours" (Mark 11:24).

This is an extraordinary promise. It is seldom realized because many prayers are phony. When the heart says one thing and the lips say another, the heart always wins. Real prayers, which represent our true inner cravings, are answered. The person who prays, "Lord, give us concern for others," and then cheats his employees is sending God mixed signals. We usually do get what we want most, but that's not always what we say out loud, or even what we think at the conscious level.

When Jesus told his disciples "about their need to pray always and not to lose heart" (Luke 18:1), he was contrasting two approaches to life's problems. To "lose heart" means to give up and slump into apathy. Therefore, if prayer is its antithesis, it must mean to persist and avidly pursue our goal.

The essence of faith is to believe in possibilities. Faith sends a "cue" to our subconscious. Faith activates deep, powerful resources, and undreamed of breakthroughs occur. Everything we've achieved as a human race has been by this principle of faith. Birds fly by instinct, but man does it by faith. He wished he could, then thought he could, then believed he could, and finally developed that belief into technology and did it!

Prayer is not hocus-pocus magic. It doesn't work like an incantation. Frederick Douglass said he often prayed for liberation, but until he put his feet into the act and ran away, his prayer was not answered. God works through us!

If asking were the whole story, why did Jesus add "search, and you will find; knock, and the door will be opened for you" (Matt 7:7)? This sounds paradoxical because he also tells us that God is more than willing to give: "How much more will your Father in heaven give good things to those who ask him!" (Matt 7:11).

If that's so, what hinders him? Why must we seek and knock? The explanation is simple. The most valuable things cannot be arbitrarily bestowed. God cannot give if we won't take!

Parents may fervently desire to give their son an education, but if the boy doesn't want one, the mother and father are helpless. One person cannot give another person integrity or discipline. These things have to be sought by the recipient. Prayers can't be answered if there's no reception. A radio station may broadcast urgent messages, but the announcer can never impart knowledge to a man who merely sits by a radio. If he won't turn it on and tune it to the appropriate frequency, nothing happens. Prayer is turning on and tuning in to God. This requires listening, understanding, and acting.

Furthermore, we must learn how to recognize God's spiritual language. An old story is told of a man waiting for a reply to a telegram. When he complained because his message had not come, the operator said, "Your message is coming. I'm receiving it right now!" The clicking and clacking meant nothing to the untrained man. It's ironic that he didn't recognize his message when he heard it! Even so, God speaks in ordinary life, but we must be prepared to recognize the message.

Self-conquest is the greatest victory that can be achieved. Through prayer, individuals eliminate unwholesome emotions. They avoid trivial irrelevancies. They replace false values with deeper interests. Constant adjustment and correction are essential.

The conflict between the desire to please God and the desire to please those who claimed to represent him was the central struggle of Jesus's life. He fought out the dilemma in prayer. His sights were set on becoming "at one" with God. To satisfy his Father was his dominant motive. To do his will was his greatest pleasure.

At the inspiring events of baptism and transfiguration, Jesus was blessed with the assurance that he was "a beloved son" in whom God was well pleased. He summed up his duty, saying, "The one who sent me is with me; he has not left me alone, for I always do what is pleasing to him" (John 8:29).

When Jesus thought of heaven and reward, he didn't dream of golden streets or pearly gates. He saw only his approving Father saying, "Well done, good and trustworthy slave" (Matt 25:21).

Even Jesus, however, had to deal with a life filled with conflict. To please God meant to displease his family. To please God meant to displease the leaders of his nation. To please God meant to displease the priests of the temple. This meant he would be deserted by his friends and opposed by his enemies. It meant he would be thought insane by his household, a traitor by his countrymen, and a heretic by the religious leaders.

Jesus's great personal battles were waged in prayer before their results were seen in public. He fought his secret war in the wilderness, in the mountains, and in the garden of Gethsemane. The scripture says, "Jesus offered up prayers and supplications, with loud cries and tears, to the one who was able to save him from death" (Heb 5:7). That sort of praying is a real struggle. It earnestly requests the ability to know and the courage to do the will of God. No life can escape that struggle if it is to achieve maturity.

Prayer is opening up your soul. God can make himself real only to the one who prays. The best things in life cannot be dropped out of heaven or draped like a mantle over a person's shoulders. Greatness of character can't be given; it must be developed! Success can't be given; it must be earned! Maturity can't be given; it must be reached through growth!

In the story of the prodigal son, we see the younger boy's progress from his first request to his last one (see Luke 15:11–13, 17–19). Before he leaves, he demands, "Give me what is mine. Let me be happy!" When he returns, he says, "Make me a servant. Let me be useful!" Which one is a better prayer? It's obvious that through his adversity he had gained maturity.

Prayer has many positive effects. It exposes the soul to God's prompting. It rouses us out of lethargy and averts us from "the path of least resistance." When our need becomes greater than our apathy and doubt, we pray. James said, "The prayer of the righteous is powerful and effective" (Jas 5:16).

Prayer shows us another world. It points us toward a higher kingdom. We're like the tadpole that finally poked its nose out of the puddle into the air above. In surprise it exclaimed, "You mean there's something else one can breathe besides water?" That was his first step toward becoming a frog. When he begins to breathe in a different atmosphere, he begins to change. So do we!

Prayer can be exhilarating, as when Jesus's face shone with glory (see Matt 17:1–6). However, these heights are not often reached.

Even the record of Jesus's life contains only one such transfiguration experience.

Prayer can be routine, as when Jesus murmured, "I knew that you always hear me" (John 11:42).

Prayer can be agonizing, as in the garden of Gethsemane: "Then he withdrew from them about a stone's throw, knelt down, and prayed.... In his anguish he prayed more earnestly, and his sweat became like great drops of blood falling down on the ground" (Luke 22:41, 44).

Each prayer experience varies, but all are worthwhile. It's axiomatic that we can't remain the same after a divine encounter. This divine encounter, however, does not consist of human beings groveling in the dust, declaring their utter worthlessness. God isn't an egotistical maniac requiring constant adoration from cringing slaves. Such destructive teachings reflect a vestige of paganism.

Many of the words and phrases used to describe the man/God relationship developed in an era of absolute monarchs and authoritatively ruled kingdoms. Thrones, scepters, commands, and decrees were common symbols. Power, might, majesty, and glory were complimentary terms. We are now in an entirely different era. Life has moved on. Civilization has improved. Masters have mostly disappeared. Tyranny is considered illegitimate.

Being "dependent" and "submissive" in an open, liberated society accomplishes very little. If democracy is better, if freedom is a right, if individuals are autonomous, then we must rethink our view of man, God, and prayer. We must change our ideas of how progress is achieved, of how goals are reached, and of how kingdoms are brought in. We've learned by experience that God won't do it for us! In fact, if he did, he'd destroy us.

There seems to be a psychological principle that "people only do what they have to do." A spoon-fed baby never matures. A child with every need provided never grows. A person with every wish fulfilled never struggles. Since maturity, growth, and struggle are necessary, it's important for prayer to reward initiative, not laziness.

Platitudes such as "depend on the Lord," "turn it all over to him," "let go and let God" have never been effective. Even in New Testament times these doctrines backfired, and Paul had to say, "Anyone unwilling to work should not eat" (2 Thess 3:10).

James knew this when he said, "Be ye doers of the word, and not hearers only" (Jas 1:22 KJV). Too often, we seem to be told that the less we do, the more God will do! That's absolutely false! Diffidence, insecurity, and timidity are not spiritual virtues.

Old Testament religious teachers and even some New Testament writers seem to encourage submissive obedience, passive hopes, and patient endurance. That's because, in their world, these characteristics and attitudes were their only options. The majority of people were limited in their opportunities for self-direction and self-expression. Most men and women occupied filial or servant roles.

While obedience, conformity, and docility may have been excellent traits for surviving in a dictatorship or a slave state, we are realizing that they are atrocious traits for building a democracy of free, responsible individuals. A submissive, passive, patient outlook sets the stage for mob rule, "sheep mentalities," and cult followings. Acquiescence develops a welfare society made up of "yes men."

It's absurd that we extol people for exemplifying blind faith, utter dependence, and a subservient lifestyle in religion and then condemn them for doing the same thing in athletics, industry, and politics. The human personality cannot be split up in this fashion without harm. We can't exemplify one personality, one set of characteristics, and one outlook in work and another in worship. We can't operate one way in the office and another in the church. With such conflicting signals it's not surprising that we are an alienated and fragmented society.

It's also evident that some prayers are used for immoral purposes. The pagan's prayer endeavors to make his god his slave. His one idea is to get what he wants. The Christian's prayer, on the other hand, must give God an opportunity to do through us what he wants to do in this world. God's will and purposes can be hindered by our unreadiness, our lack of receptivity, our closed hearts, and our unresponsive minds. God probably observes our lives like Jesus observed Jerusalem when he said, "How often have I desired…and you were not willing!" (Matt 23:37).

Now, why didn't the young family with the abusive father have their prayers answered? Why wasn't the attractive man with great potential converted? If we will not, God cannot! What a position we hold! What a role we play! What a responsibility we have!

Thinking

A certain mother and son had a special relationship. They were both sensitive, artistic, and intelligent. They also shared a love for poetry, painting, and music. The little boy sometimes had trouble adjusting to life because, although he had a gift for language, he wasn't very good at sports. On those occasions when he had difficult social experiences, he could always confide in his mother. She was both confidant and friend.

When he was ten years old, however, his mother became very ill. She tired easily and felt generally rundown. Eventually, she was diagnosed as having leukemia, a deadly form of cancer. The nightmare began. There were only a few months left to prepare. Everything a mother hopes to pass on during a lifetime—all the wisdom and companionship—had to be compressed into less than a year.

Both parent and child were devastated. When long nights came and sleep was impossible, they talked and cried and imagined the unfulfilled dreams of the future. A thousand hopes were expressed. A hundred bits of advice were articulated. Youthful plans for a vocation in the ministry were laid. A profound sense of responsibility developed.

The day after school was out in the spring, death came. The father tried to fill the gap, but the common bond of interest, the emotional compatibility, the mutual understanding were missing. As a result, a unique individual with an unusual array of personal gifts was lost. The young man never reached his potential. His capabilities were largely untapped. He became an undisciplined drifter, without focus and purpose.

Now, during the months of her illness, this Christian mother's church, family, and friends had prayed unceasingly for her recovery. Many sincere intercessions pointed out to God, time and time again, that her child needed her desperately. They were right. He did need her!

Is it possible God didn't know that? Wasn't he aware that not only her life but her talented son's life would be wasted by this tragedy? Why didn't he intervene? Why didn't he make some scientist discover a useful medication? Why didn't he cause some doctor to administer a successful remedy? In fact, there are several chemotherapies now available that might have prolonged her life. Why couldn't they have been developed a few years earlier?

Well, they could have been if everyone with technical and creative ability had lived up to their potential. The reason the drugs and procedures were not there when this woman needed them is because men and women on this earth had failed to develop them.

God can't circumvent humanity. He can't make end runs around us in order to accomplish his purposes. He has to use our minds and our energies. He cannot force insights or superimpose information. His gift of human freedom constrains his actions.

God can't endow us with knowledge. It can only be learned through personal study and research. Solomon said, "I turned my mind to know and to search out and to seek wisdom and the sum of things" (Eccl 7:25).

The idea that God can do everything—that he can work his will without any response from us—is false! God's will and purpose depend upon human cooperation! God cannot do some things unless individuals learn, think, and discover! He never emblazons his truth across the sky in plain English so that people may find it without seeking. It's only when we give ourselves to intellectual toil that God can reveal truths about the physical or spiritual world!

God can't make people think something against their wills. Jesus said, "Ask, and it will be given to you; search, and you will find; knock, and the door will be opened for you. For everyone who asks receives, and everyone who searches finds, and for everyone who knocks, the door will be opened" (Luke 11:9–10).

It's significant that Jesus said, "Ask, seek, and knock." This advocates an orderly process. Now, some things can come by simply asking. In certain cases, merely stating our need and determining a feasible course of action is enough. Some problems involving family or economic conditions can be solved if God is allowed to stir up our subconscious memories and inspire wisdom. Obviously, other problems—like finding a cure for cancer—require much more! By differentiating between types of problems, Jesus definitely insinuates that prayers don't consist of getting God to push a magic button. If this were the case, then one thing is no harder than another with God.

The next step, *seek*, might be translated *research* in modern language. It means to search, to inquire, to look for something hidden. Scientists who patiently explore options and analyze causes are seeking. Seeking requires patience, perseverance, and personal deprivation.

In fact, several scriptures refer to both fasting and prayer when facing difficult situations (see Luke 2:37; Acts 13:2; Acts 14:23). What is fasting? Is it simply doing without food? No! It's any form of voluntary abstinence. It is giving up ordinary satisfactions, pleasures, and luxuries to devote ourselves wholeheartedly to our pursuits. Madame Curie—in a dark basement, cut off from friends, social affairs, and fashionable clothes—was fasting. Thomas Edison—spending twenty hours a day in a dreary workshop—was fasting. Astronauts—who deny themselves the comforts of family and home for long periods of time—are fasting!

The final step, *knock*, means to be determined, to remove obstacles, and to keep trying until the door of success opens.

What, then, does God's commitment to our mental freedom have to do with prayer? For one thing, it defines the meaning of inspiration. Inspiration doesn't supernaturally impart secret knowledge to a lazy mind. It doesn't arbitrarily implant information into an ignorant mind.

Inspiration must work through the ordinary experiences the person has had. It must use the natural processes of the human brain. It can raise our awareness to a high degree and urge us to develop understandings, but it can't cause us to know things we have not tried to learn. That would reward inertia. Inspiration can help us realize our possibilities and reach our potential, but it can't impute unrelated details or bestow undeveloped skills out of a clear blue sky. That would undermine human freedom.

God's response to our petitions is contingent upon our mental state. Insights may seem to come in a flash. Inspiration may suddenly illuminate us. An idea may be born instantaneously. Newton's concept of gravity, Einstein's theory of relativity, and Edison's application of electricity each may have culminated in a moment, but they weren't developed in a moment. Intellectual breakthroughs don't happen to unprepared minds. Someday we may discover that revelation is simply one special kind of reasoning.

Jesus emphasized sincerity in prayer because the answer is totally dependent upon it. This means the petition offered must be the genuine expression of an inward desire. The fault of the Pharisees who prayed on the street corners was not that they were asking for unworthy things. Their petitions were doubtlessly excellent, springing out of scriptural ideas and couched in religious language, but the prayers did not represent the true inward desires of the men who prayed. The petitions were not sincere. We must work for the same things we pray for. The lives of the Pharisees blatantly advertised that their real ambitions did not agree with their sanctimonious supplications.

We pray as we think we ought to. We ask for the blessings we feel are proper. We plead for graces we believe we should want, whether we do or not. We mask ourselves behind a veneer. Disguised in religious clothes, we ask God for the things we presume God wants us to ask for.

However, our outward prayers must match our inward prayers, or all is in vain. We see clearly that many of the speeches addressed to God are not real prayers at all. They are not our dominant desires.

They do not express the inward direction and determination of our lives. What we pray for in the closet is not the thing we persistently seek in the marketplace.

When we say "God give me understanding" but then choose to spend our spare time in the bowling alley rather than the library, the incongruity is revealed. When we say "God make me holy" but then run our business in an unethical way, the incongruity is revealed.

Prayer that is not our dominant desire is too weak to achieve anything. Any lazy student can pray to be educated. Any idler on a park bench can pray to be rich. Any dodger of duty can pray for success. However, such "praying" is not really prayer.

Perseverance is the secret. Jesus told a parable about prayer: "Suppose one of you has a friend, and you go to him at midnight and say to him, 'Friend, lend me three loaves of bread, for a friend of mine has arrived, and I have nothing to set before him.' And he answers from within, 'Do not bother me; the door has already been locked, and my children are with me in bed; I cannot get up and give you anything.' I tell you, even though he will not get up and give him anything out of friendship, at lease because of his persistence he will get up and give him whatever he needs" (Luke 11:5–8).

Now, the purpose of this parable is not to describe a reluctant and uncaring god. Instead, the purpose is to encourage half-hearted and impatient people who give up too soon.

The key phrase here is *because of his persistence*. You see, life is set up to reward dogged determination. Too often we lack that eagerness to receive, which reveals itself in earnest prayer. This note of urgency is heard in Jacob's wrestling with the angel when he said, "I will not let you go, unless you bless me" (Gen 32:26). Such urgency is often lacking in our supplication. In fact, these demands may sound irreverent, but they are effective!

When we see Copernicus questioning the heavens year after year to discover the truth or watch Peary as he tried undauntedly to reach the unexplored polar regions, we catch at least a faint idea of the necessity of prayer. "For twenty-four years," Peary said, "sleeping or awake, to place the Stars and Stripes on the Pole had been my dream." That is the spirit of seeking, which leads to fulfillment, and that is the spirit of prayer. Those who possess these attributes will not be denied.

Now, that young mother with leukemia died. That gifted son's life was ruined because over the years all those individuals with medical and scientific gifts had not been sufficiently dedicated to discover the causes and cure of blood diseases. The prayers may have been asked, but the persistent commitments of seeking and knocking were missing. Those people through whom God could have answered that prayer had not made themselves available. Intellectually endowed men and women refused to be channels of God's healing process.

Apathetic humanity, not God, failed! God hates cancer as much as we do. The fact that Jesus stood adamantly against disease proves which side God is on! His constant concern for hurting people overturned forever the old belief that suffering is God's punishment! Being a Christian is to be an agent for change in this world. It is to be the hands, the feet, the mouth, the heart, and the mind through which God acts!

Doing

A talented young college couple worked in a small church close to their campus. For two years they directed music, visited, and organized children's choirs. The struggling congregation had grave financial problems and even worse leadership problems. The elderly, almost illiterate pastor alienated the student community and finally scandalized the entire town by having an affair with one of his young parishioners.

After this disgraceful episode occurred, the little church practically folded, but the ministerial student and his wife, who had just graduated, had a dream. They visualized a dynamic program designed to reach the nearby university area. They had unique gifts for the challenge with majors in speech, drama, and music. The salary would be negligible, but that didn't matter. They were willing to work and live in low-rent housing until the church could get back on its feet. This was surely God's will. Everything fit! The timing was perfect. For once the obvious needs meshed exactly with the available abilities. They prayed and felt complete assurance that this was their place of service, but it didn't happen!

The congregation loved and appreciated the couple but decided to call an older, more experienced man. This decision was not productive. The new pastor didn't work out. The church never recovered. It never revived. It never reached its potential. The college clientele was not served. The church struggled for a year or two, hurt many people both in and out of the congregation, and finally disbanded.

Nobody won in this situation. The young couple were denied an outlet for their enthusiasm at a crucial point in their lives, and the church failed in its mission. The preacher and his wife had felt led—had made a commitment. Why didn't God answer?

To understand such complexities we must realize that God's gift of human freedom constrains his action. God can't make people do something against their will. In the scriptures God said, "I held out my hands all day long to a rebellious people, who walk in a way that is not good, following their own devices.... When I called, you did not answer, when I spoke, you did not listen, but you did what was evil in my sight and chose what I did not delight in" (Isa 65:2, 12).

In this case, God couldn't rig the vote. The congregation chose, and even though it was a wrong choice, God was bound to honor their right to make it! He can't override our personal inclinations and force us to make valid decisions. The liberty of conscience is total! There are no exceptions. God let Israel say "No!" The scriptures say, "In returning and rest you shall be saved; in quietness and in trust shall be your strength. But you refused and said, 'No!'" (Isa 30:15–16). Jesus also respected individual preferences. He allowed the rich young ruler to walk away (see Luke 18:18–24). He let the entire city of Jerusalem exercise their rights of rejection (see Matt 23:37).

Some people say, "God is sovereign! He's in control of every aspect of life!" Who are they kidding? We know it's God's will that all people should repent and claim abundant life. If that's true, then why don't they? Because they have the freedom to refuse. We know it was Jesus's desire to perform great deeds in Nazareth. If that's true, then why didn't he? Because they had the freedom to disbelieve. The decision to affirm our spiritual responsibilities is an individual matter for us, even as it was for Joshua, who fortunately made the right choice, saying, "As for me and my household, we will serve the LORD" (Josh 24:15).

Likewise, the decision to deny our spiritual possibilities is an individual matter for us, even as it was for the Hebrews. The scripture says, "They refused to listen and turned a stubborn shoulder and stopped their ears in order not to hear" (Zech 7:11).

Now, what does our freedom of action have to do with answers to prayers? It has everything to do with them, because God cannot do some things without human hands. This is obvious in everyday life. When God wants bridges and tunnels constructed, when God wants a cathedral built, does he do the work himself? Of course not! Such expectations reveal an absurd and idle fatalism. God stocked the hills with marble, but he never built a Parthenon. God filled the mountains with ore, but he never made a needle. Only when people work can some things be done. Even God can't fill the role that was meant for me!

Furthermore, if God sends blessings arbitrarily, apart from our own initiative and energy, then we'd have to conclude that he also sends tragedies arbitrarily, apart from our own negligence and errors. Intelligent individuals and deep thinkers are greatly disturbed by these incongruous claims.

Some things never come without thinking. Some things never come without working. Some things never come without praying! Prayer is one aspect of a person's cooperation with God. It links us up with divine intelligence. It connects us with divine power. It's not our passive resignation to God's will that leads to progress. Instead, it's our active cooperation with God's will that accomplishes great things. The doers of this world are not resigned. They see an arid desert, and far from being resigned, they irrigate it into lush productivity. They see a thorny cactus, and far from being resigned, they use modern horticultural discoveries to make it into a beneficial food source. They see social evils like discrimination and slavery, and far from being resigned, they devote all their strength to eradicate them. Resignation in the presence of evil is sin!

God is constantly trying to help us answer our own requests. We ask for things, and God's answer is to supply enough wisdom for us to get them. Almost any petition can be answered if God can get the right thoughts into the minds of the right men and women. Suppose we need a job. If God can put an appropriate suggestion into our mind or a potential employer's mind or into both of our minds, the prayer can be answered. This is done by means of—not in spite of—the laws of mental action.

Consider what this world would become if everything could be accomplished by merely asking. What if captains could sail their ships as well by prayer alone as by knowledge of the science of navigation? What if engineers could build their bridges as effectively by petition only as by studying the principles of engineering? What if families could light their homes, send their messages, and feed their children by mere entreaty, rather than by technological advances and hard work?

Isn't it obvious that if we had the power of wishing conferred upon us, as described in fairytales, we'd never use our intelligence or our energy? Since the purpose of life is to encourage the development of human beings, then our own thoughts and actions, as well as prayer, are absolutely necessary in order to achieve results.

If a boy asks his father to do his homework because he wants to play, should the father do it? The father loves the boy. He can easily work the problems and diagram the sentences, but that boy's verbal prayer must never be allowed to substitute for his own physical and mental exertion. The father, in answer to the boy's request, may encourage him, assist him, stand by him, and see him through, but the father must not do anything for his son that the son can do for himself.

Too many prayers attempt to accomplish by supplication what can only be accomplished by work. In one of the most dramatic scenes in the exodus, the Israelites are caught with the formidable Red Sea in front of them and the angry Egyptians behind them. At this moment Moses stops to pray. The reply he receives is startling. It is almost a rebuke for having prayed! The scripture says, "Then the LORD said to Moses, 'Why do you cry out to me? Tell the Israelites to go forward'" (Exod 14:15).

It is as though God were saying, "I have everything ready, but nothing can be done until you take advantage of it. It's your move!" Never before has it so clearly and urgently been our move. This generation has searching questions. It has an honest unwillingness to act without knowledge. It refuses to accept assurance without good reason. This outlook forces us to examine intercessory prayer. The confusion may lie in the inadequate definition of *intercession*.

Too often, theology concerning prayer has been expressed to insinuate that a sincere, caring Christian has to persuade a thoughtless or unwilling God to do something for someone else. This dishonors God, invades the other person's freedom, and insults our intelligence.

God cannot save my family without my cooperation because he cannot take my place as son or husband or father. He must work through me! God cannot save my country without my cooperation because he cannot take my place as a soldier or voter or public official. He must work through me. God cannot save the lost without my cooperation because he cannot take my place as a witness or visitor or missionary. He must work through me! There is nothing irreverent about emphasizing the necessity of human cooperation. It is God's plan for the ages. It defines mankind's role in the eternal scheme of things.

The church we described failed and folded because the members made some wrong decisions. God wasn't in charge of that situation—the human congregation was! Their freedom to act was absolute!

Conclusion

Prayer is one of the most misunderstood doctrines in religion today. Prayer is also one of the most often abused practices in religion today. Numerous news stories and headlines reveal some problem or some crisis that involves our definition of prayer. From tragedies to miracles, we are facing a world that puts an ever-increasing strain on our theological assumptions: Why do mass shootings occur? Why do earthquakes wipe out cities? Why do we have disease, crime, and wars? These questions are real and relevant.

A magical, wand-waving God simply won't fit with the facts. If God is in charge, why do so many tragic senseless things happen? People can accept a natural death at the end of a long life, but wholesale massacres and the torture of children raise questions. A God of integrity can't be cruel or careless.

This theological crisis has increased in the twenty-first century because our world has become much smaller. In this generation we literally see it all. Television has brought unspeakable atrocities into our living rooms. The internet has opened our lives to the pain of people all over the world. A recent national poll inquired, "If you could ask God one question, what would it be?" The subjects evil, suffering, and war topped the list.

A baby is born with a horrible genetic defect. A bright child is killed in an automobile accident. A young mother is blinded by a rare disease. An elderly person lingers for months in a painful dying condition. Such tragedies happen constantly. Such tragedies have always happened constantly.

Until very recently, these kinds of disorders and misfortunes were almost universally assumed to have been caused by God. They were considered to be punishments or tests or lessons. Things are beginning to change. As scientific knowledge expands to include causes and effects, the absolute senselessness of many evils is seen as incongruous with a God of truth.

As ethical development progresses, the totally indiscriminate nature of many evils is seen as incompatible with a God of righteousness. As communication possibilities increase, the sheer overwhelming magnitude of evil and suffering is seen as incongruous with Jesus's God of love.

Christians, caught off guard as usual when it comes to deep theological matters, retreat, saying, "Well, maybe God doesn't actually cause it, but he allows it! His permissive will overrides his purposeful will." What a copout!

This stance is fast becoming just as ludicrous as the former because logical thinkers realize that if God can prevent evil or suffering and doesn't, he's just as culpable as if he caused it! If a lifeguard saved one person and deliberately let five others drown, he'd be considered a murderer. This claim is unthinkable! It's unbelievable! It's immoral, yet it permeates all of life!

An Olympic skier broke her leg and said, "I think everything happens for a reason. I needed time to rest!" This insinuation is invalid. God doesn't break legs. Now, the athlete did make the best of it and maybe even used it to her advantage, but to claim that God causes any evil is ridiculous. James said, "Every generous act of giving, with every perfect gift, is from above, coming down from the Father of lights, with whom there is no variation or shadow due to change" (James 1:17).

The problem of God's sovereignty and human suffering can be illustrated by considering an analogy: Parents let a child learn to walk, knowing full well there will be bumps and falls and pain. They do this because the alternative would be paralysis. The failures are part of the process, but the parents certainly don't put obstacles in the way! They certainly don't knock the baby down. They certainly don't deliberately trip him. That's crazy!

If a child fell over an obstacle on the floor and said, "Everything happens for a reason. Mom must have put that there to punish me for disobeying her this morning," we'd say, "Nuts!" If a child said, "Everything happens for a reason. Mom must have put that there to test me to see if I'll still love her even if she hurts me," we'd say, "Nuts!" If a child said, "Everything happens for a reason. Mom must have put that there to trip me so I'll learn how to get up," we'd say, "Nuts!"

Now, the fall does happen for a reason. It has a cause: immature muscles, poor balance, and lack of experience. Plus, the accidental confrontation with an obstacle causes the fall. Furthermore, the child does strengthen muscles, learn balance, and develop persistence through falls, but they are not good in and of themselves. They are not the will of the parent! Theoretically, if the child's muscles were strong, his balance perfect, and his determination adequate, then he'd never fall! He'd never need to fall! That would be the ideal.

On a practical level we know muscles aren't strong, balance isn't perfect, and determination isn't adequate at first. Therefore, falls occur, not caused by God, not arbitrarily allowed by God, but as part of the process of growth.

Likewise, if a Christian meets adversity or sorrow and says, "Everything happens for a reason. God must have caused this to punish me for some disobedience," we must say, "Nuts!" Likewise, if a Christian meets adversity and sorrow and says, "Everything happens for a reason, God must have caused this to test my faith," we must say, "Nuts!" Likewise, if a Christian meets adversity and sorrow and says, "Everything happens for a reason. God must have caused this so I'll become stronger," we must say, "Nuts!"

Now, the adversity or sorrow does happen for a reason. It does have a cause: human ignorance, weakness, and inertia. Plus, confrontation with life's obstacles causes the misfortune. Furthermore, Christians can learn, grow, and mature through such misfortunes, but they are not good in and of themselves. They are not the will of God! Theoretically, if mankind had perfect knowledge, abilities, and will, we'd never have any problems. That's the ideal.

On a practical level we know our knowledge, abilities, and will are not perfect. There are plenty of things in this life to cause people to stumble, but anyone who would deliberately create such snares is evil and guilty! Jesus gave this exact explanation, saying, "Woe to the world because of things that cause sin! Such things are bound to come, but woe to the one through they come!" (Matt 18:7).

It's inevitable that tragedies will occur—not caused by God, not arbitrarily allowed by God, but as part of the process called life.

Understandings in this area are important because modern Christians need a reasonable, ethical belief system from which to exercise their faith. Sooner or later, we must realize that divine omnipotence is not absolute. God has constraints upon his sovereignty. When we say this, we're not being irreverent; we're just being realistic.

God's character limits his actions. Anyone can see that things that are true and things that are false are mutually exclusive. If God exemplifies truth, then prayers like that of the little girl who said, "Please, God, make Boston the capitol of Vermont, because that's what I put on my test paper," can't be answered.

Anyone can see that actions that are fair and actions that are unfair are mutually exclusive. If God exemplifies righteousness, then prayers like that of a smoker with lung cancer, who begs, "Please, God, make an exception in my case," can't be answered.

Anyone can see that methods that are constructive and methods that are destructive are mutually exclusive. If God exemplifies love, then prayers like that of a lazy student, who parties all night and then pleads, "Please, God, do my test for me, just this once," can't be answered.

God's natural principles limit his actions. Anyone can see that systems that are compatible and systems that are incompatible are mutually exclusive. If natural principles are unified, then prayers like that of the hopeless skier who looks up at the blue sky and prays, "Please, God, make it snow," can't be answered.

Anyone can see that laws that are dependable and laws that are undependable are mutually exclusive. If natural principles are consistent, then prayers like that of the falling mountain climber who screams, "Please God, suspend the law of gravity for ten minutes," can't be answered.

Anyone can see that practices that are productive and practices that are nonproductive are mutually exclusive. If natural principles are progressive, then prayers like that of the careless gardener who says, "Please, God, I know I planted crabgrass, but let flowers come up instead," can't be answered.

God's gift of human freedom limits his actions. Anyone can see that forcing people into robotic forms and allowing people to become what they choose are mutually exclusive. If mankind's freedom "to be" is absolute, then prayers like that of the girl in love who says, "Please, God, make my fiancé want to go to Hawaii on our honeymoon," can't he answered.

Anyone can see that forcing people to think certain thoughts or to repeat certain words and allowing people to express their own opinions are mutually exclusive. If mankind's freedom in thought and speech is absolute, then prayers like that of the teenager who begs, "Please, God, make the captain of the football team call me for a date," can't be answered.

Anyone can see that forcing people to react like puppets on a string and allowing them to respond voluntarily are mutually exclusive. If mankind's "freedom to act" is absolute, then prayers like that of the worker who says, "Please, God, make my employer give me a raise," can't be answered.

In considering the constraints imposed by God's character, God's natural principles, and mankind's freedom, we need to realize that God acts on an overall and long-term basis. This insight assures us that God "pre-answers" most prayers by building remedies and solutions into the very scheme of things. The scripture says, "Before they call I will answer" (Isa 65:24). In fact, answers are already within the system, merely waiting to be activated by our perceptive understanding and correct action.

Achieving success in many endeavors can be compared to the operation of an automatic door. It won't open until you approach. No amount of pleading or shouting will affect the mechanism. It's set to open in one particular way. When we do the right thing, get in the right position, and make the right move, it works and not until!

Likewise, no amount of begging, persuading, promising, or bribing will affect the natural sequence of actions and consequences in this life. The universe is set to operate in a particular way. Certain causes produce certain effects. When we do the right thing, get in the right position, and make the right move, our life works and not until.

Illustrations of God's "pre-answers" are commonplace. Suppose a tree branch falls on a child and the mother prays frantically, "God, give me strength to remove it." In fact, this petition may be unnecessary. She probably already has the strength. God and nature have programmed us for emergencies. The adrenalin, the hormones, and the other chemical and biological reinforcements are there inside her. She simply has to exert herself to utilize these powers.

This may explain why many of Jesus's wondrous deeds were based on commands, not prayers. It's significant that he told his disciples to order the mountain removed. He didn't say, "Beg God to move the mountain" (see Matt 17:20).

Indeed, we have the essential instincts, the subconscious knowledge, and the extraordinary energies within ourselves to meet most of life's crises. Our bodies heal themselves. Our emotions adapt to change. Our minds invent and create solutions as needs arise.

It's important to note, however, that both believers and unbelievers, both people who pray and people who don't pray, have these marvelous resources. If that's true, many people rightly ask, "Then what's the use of praying?" The honest reply is "None" if we're using prayer to persuade God to override his reluctance or to change his mind!

Prayer doesn't change God; it changes us! Prayer clears our mind of preconceptions. Prayer focuses our mental powers. Prayer verbalizes our deepest desires. Prayer taps into our subconscious store of knowledge. Prayer releases our latent abilities. Prayer revives our idle energies. In short, prayer activates those dormant possibilities and reveals those hidden answers. Therefore, prayer is eminently legitimate and worthwhile, even though there are petitions God can't answer!

Saying there are petitions God can't answer and things God can't do shouldn't upset us. It should reassure us. If God, in the beginning, created order out of chaos; if God, in the beginning, set this universe into organized motion; if God, in the beginning, ordained certain purposes, then we obviously cannot expect him to change the rules now in the middle of the game.

What God has done is done right; it doesn't need any midflight corrections. What God has done is done permanently; it doesn't have to be strengthened or improved. Solomon said, "I know that whatever God does endures forever; nothing can be added to it nor anything taken from it; God has done this so that all should stand in awe before him" (Eccl 3:14).

This doesn't mean God made the world and then abandoned it! On the contrary, there is constant divine/human interaction! He seeks to reveal, and we seek to perceive. This theological situation may be explained in a simple analogy: One contractor builds a home, and a family moves in. They camp in the middle of the room, living in a crude manner, eating sandwiches and sleeping in bags on the floor. When they get cold in winter, they frantically call up the contractor, who after some deliberation comes out and brings a camp stove. When they get hot in summer, they frantically call up the contractor, who reluctantly brings out a small fan! Often, however, as needs arise, they aren't able to reach the contractor and therefore have to make do or live at a substandard level. All in all, it's not a very satisfactory arrangement!

Another contractor builds a home, and a family moves in. Unlike the other residents, this family is not content to camp or eat sandwiches or sleep on the floor. They have faith in their contractor. They firmly believe he has provided for every contingency. Therefore, they set out to learn all about their dwelling place. They find buttons, wires, and mechanical aids. Every day a new labor-saving device is discovered. When an emergency arises, such as a blizzard, they too call their contractor, but he says, "It's already there. Your need was anticipated, and the resources to meet those needs were preinstalled." He gives instructions, and the efficient furnace is activated. In summer the air conditioner is activated.

This contractor doesn't have to keep dashing out to remedy some fault, to modify some system, or to improve his creation. It's all been done. The original plans were complete. The construction was perfect! Nothing is lacking! The family only has to discover and learn how to use what is already available!

Now, which contractor was superior?

One person says, "I trust my contractor. I am completely dependent upon him. He will rush in and bail me out if the plumbing breaks, if the electricity fails, or if I need an appliance in an emergency."

Another says, "I trust my contractor, but I don't expect him to rush in and bail me out. It's not because he isn't capable of doing so, but because he doesn't need to. He built it right in the first place. Furthermore, he didn't want to keep me dependent. He wanted to challenge my initiative! Every one of my needs was foreseen, but it's up to me to discover these marvelous devices and utilize them."

Which occupant is more likely to mature into responsible autonomy? Which occupant is more likely to grow and become independent? Which occupant is more likely to live a productive and abundant life?

A mature Christian tries to understand the process. A mature Christian tries to discover proper methods. A mature Christian tries to trigger desired responses. These activities require an active faith, not a passive credulity. This kind of living faith declares there is a way to solve problems. This kind of living faith maintains there is a way to achieve good.

Neither faith nor prayer, however, is a spiritual "open sesame" guaranteed to grant all wishes. In fact, there is evidence that even Jesus's prayers were not always answered. He did say, "I knew that you always hear me" (John 11:42), but there are still questions. For instance, didn't Jesus pray for the rich young ruler, the city of Jerusalem, and Judas? Yet they all rejected him and his message. Also, what about his prayer from the cross? "Father, forgive them" (Luke 23:34). Did this petition effect a wholesale pardon for all those participating in the crucifixion?

What we must realize is that intercession requires two consents, or else the free will of those prayed for would be violated! It's significant that Jesus told his disciples to pray for the harvesters, not the harvest. He said to pray for strength to witness, not for sinners to repent.

Perhaps the reason lies in the area of human freedom. God can't force or coerce unbelievers. Therefore, persuasion is his only tool. If a person has no spiritual affiliation, then God can't persuade him. If a person is unattuned, then God can't influence him.

Christians, on the other hand, do have that spiritual affinity. They can be persuaded. So prayers for workers to witness can be effective. Those who are attuned can be influenced. God can "send forth harvesters" if those being commissioned are willing to receive the divine message and obey the divine urge. God can only work through those who are committed.

We're not to wait for answers; we're to *be* answers. The son of a wealthy man heard his pious father pray, "God, please feed the hungry and heal the sick!"

The child began to pull at his father's coat. After a hasty "Amen," the irate parent said, "Now, what did you want?"

"Well, I was going to tell you," the boy replied, "that if you will give me your checkbook for five minutes, I'll answer your prayer."

It's up to us! Traditional explanations and unrealistic expectations concerning God's role in the universe are detrimental to society.

First, these explanations do a great disservice to God. In a world full of inequities, the Creator is presented as either an unfeeling monster or an inept manager!

Second, these explanations lay a heavy burden of guilt on both the victims and their fellow Christians. Those who suffer think, "What did I do to deserve this? I must be a very bad person!" Christians worry, "Maybe if I had only prayed more or had more faith, I could have persuaded God to avert this tragedy."

Third, these explanations distort and twist our reasoning system. We must have moral consonance, and trying to fit every tragedy to an appropriate sin causes dishonesty and inner resentment. Furthermore, once you've shifted your brain into false, shallow grooves, it's almost impossible to repair the damage.

Fourth, these explanations distract people from finding the real causes for evil. As long as you think plagues can be caused by taking a census (see 2 Sam 24:10–15), you won't do research into the habits of rats. As long as you think babies die because their parents were promiscuous, you won't discover genetic flaws or study infant mortality patterns. As long as you think touching a sacred object causes a stroke, you won't suspect eating habits or high blood pressure. As long as you think women suffer and die in childbirth because Eve ate an apple, no claims about dirty hands and bacteria will be believed.

Unfortunately, it was only when a few brave individuals dared to defy religious theology, often on pain of excommunication or death, that science and medicine leaped forward. It's ironic that it actually took a secular age of enlightenment to put Jesus's gospel into practice.

Misunderstandings impede progress and stifle growth. It's only as we begin to understand the nature of God's character, the system of natural principles, and the promise of mankind's freedom that our prayers can become less erratic and more productive. As we begin to understand the constraints these axioms place on divine sovereignty, we can become less bitter and more creative at those inevitable times when God can't answer!

www.ingramcontent.com/pod-product-compliance
Lightning Source LLC
Chambersburg PA
CBHW071009160426
43193CB00012B/1975